Rebuilding
the
ALTAR

Rebuilding the ALTAR

PAT AND KAREN SCHATZLINE

CHARISMA
HOUSE

REBUILDING THE ALTAR by Pat and Karen Schatzline
Published by Charisma House
Charisma Media/Charisma House Book Group
600 Rinehart Road
Lake Mary, Florida 32746
www.charismahouse.com

Cover design by Justin Evans

Visit the authors' websites at rebuildingthealtar.com and www.raisetheremnant.com.

Library of Congress Cataloging-in-Publication Data:
An application to register this book for cataloging has been submitted to the Library of Congress.
International Standard Book Number: 978-1-62999-146-7
E-book ISBN: 978-1-62999-147-4

17 18 19 20 21 — 9 8 7 6 5 4 3 2 1
Printed in the United States of America

The world is stampeding toward the seeker-sensitive kingdom of self. It's time for a course correction to the kingdom of God! This book will make you normal according to the Bible to carry His glory in this last day revival.

—SID ROTH
HOST, *IT'S SUPERNATURAL!*
CHARLOTTE, NORTH CAROLINA

Have you seen or felt a "shift" in the world? In your church? In your own life and spirit? Do you feel a compelling desire of passion drawing you closer to the Lord, crying out: "More, Lord?" If you answered a resounding yes to these questions, *Rebuilding the Altar* is not only a book but also a way of life that Pat and Karen Schatzline have literally woven their souls and spirits with the written Word of God to help every person who reads and studies it to become "altared" for God. As I read, the words became alive. I highly recommend this book that will catapult you deeper and higher than you've ever gone before with God. One way you can achieve this is to become "altared" by rebuilding the altar in your life!

—JIM BAKKER
FOUNDER OF PTL NETWORK, MORNINGSIDE MINISTRIES,
AND *THE JIM BAKKER SHOW*
BRANSON, MISSOURI

Rebuilding the Altar is a fresh call to personal intimacy with the Lord. I have found in my own life that there is a constant need to keep altering my walk with God. Many Christians today have settled for less in their walk with God. They swim in a small pond when the ocean is around the corner. They give up. They stop short. They sit in the sun and splash in the shallow water not knowing that just around the corner is the presence and power of God. Pat and Karen say it this way: "The key to being altered is the altar." I pray and believe that this book will lead you into a fresh and intimate relationship with our master, Jesus Christ. Pat and Karen are laying it all down on the altar. This book will inspire you to do the same.

—WARD SIMPSON
CEO, GOD TV
ALTAMONTE SPRINGS, FLORIDA

It is my great joy to recommend this book by my dear friends Pat and Karen Schatzline. I pray that you will be stirred as you hear the cry and the passion of their hearts to see revival and an awakening in America.

—DR. RODNEY HOWARD-BROWNE
EVANGELIST, REVIVAL MINISTRIES INTERNATIONAL
TAMPA, FLORIDA

Most genuine followers of Jesus Christ in America would have to admit that the church is no longer a powerful influence in shaping the direction of this country. But that can be changed. Secularism has grown to the point where the Christian message is more and more being silenced through intimidation and even outright hostility. I believe Pat and Karen Schatzline have found a way to plug back into the power we have departed from—we need "altared" people to restore spiritual and moral clarity to this nation. Pat and Karen's book gives us a portal through which the Almighty God can flow down to us and then out through us. See how the altar affects a relationship and produces change!

—MARCUS D. LAMB
FOUNDER AND PRESIDENT
DAYSTAR TELEVISION NETWORK
BEDFORD, TEXAS

The ministry of Pat and Karen Schatzline can be described in one word: *altar*. This book addresses a subject by two individuals who live their lives daily at God's altar. Pat and Karen's anointing has witnessed shattered dreams renewed again, lives torn apart restored to wholeness, and failures replaced with hope. Every time Pat and Karen Schatzline give an altar call, they rebuild an altar in someone's heart. This is one of the most powerful aspects of their ministry. Christian America can be rebuilt by restoring the altar.

—GLEN BERTEAU
SENIOR PASTOR, THE HOUSE
MODESTO, CALIFORNIA

Pat and Karen Schatzline are living examples of this book. A true wake-up call for all of us who desire a deeper, richer walk with God, *Rebuilding the Altar* will take you on a journey to know God and His purpose for your life.

—STEVE SMOTHERSON SR.
SENIOR PASTOR, LEGACY CHURCH
ALBUQUERQUE, NEW MEXCO

Pat and Karen Schatzline speak my language as they call on believers everywhere to rebuild the altars of personal devotion and to encounter the living God in a fresh new way. In ancient Israel it was a law that the fire on the altar could never go out, yet all too often, in our own walks with the Lord, that holy fire gets extinguished. That's why Pat and Karen write with such passion and conviction, pointing us back to that place of divine encounter and giving us a vision for our own lives, for our families and churches, and for the nation as a whole. It's time for a fresh awakening!

—DR. MICHAEL L. BROWN
PRESIDENT, FIRE SCHOOL OF MINISTRY
HOST, *THE LINE OF FIRE*
CHARLOTTE, NORTH CAROLINA

This is a book for this time! Evangelists Patrick and Karen Schatzline courageously brought to us this theme of rebuilding the altar, which is so necessary and foundational. In these times of changing values we need anchors that maintain our covenant with the truth. This book will certainly challenge you to live a lifestyle that burns for the presence of God, even in this world of darkness, and to be an altar upon which the flame never goes out.

—PASTOR MARCO PEIXOTO
FOUNDER AND PRESIDENT, CEIZS MINISTRIES
RIO DE JANEIRO, BRAZIL

This book's title, *Rebuilding the Altar*, conjures up many pictures in my mind—pictures of myself crying out to God around an altar as a young man and as a senior pastor for the last thirty years seeing people come to the altar at the conclusion of almost every church service. Yes, I believe it's time for every church to rebuild the place of repentance, deliverance, and recommitment to Christ.

—CARL STEPHENS
LEAD PASTOR, FAITH ASSEMBLY OF GOD
ORLANDO, FLORIDA

Today we face a world in chaos, confusion, violence, and prejudice, and mired in a spirit of division that is attempting to tear us apart in every area of life. We see churches, just like the Laodicean church, operating in a lifestyle of compromise and lukewarmness that is totally hypocritical and foreign to the teachings of Jesus and the apostles. It is a lifestyle completely contrary to the powerful and victorious life that Jesus established for us to live through and by the Holy Spirit! If you're hungry and thirsty for a fresh revelation, revival, a supernatural encounter with the Holy Spirit, and a powerful, transformed life, then this book, *Rebuilding the Altar*, is a new well to drink from and an opportunity to dine on fresh manna from heaven's oven! Be careful—this book is combustible and could set you on fire for the kingdom!

—Al Brice
Pastor, Covenant Love Church
Fayetteville, North Carolina

The Schatzlines are my covenant friends, and while we do not have the liberty to meet as regularly as we want to, each time we do, there is such a bond, one that I can only describe as a kingdom connection. This book is a rallying call for all believers, young and old, to step up in our personal prayer walk in order to fulfill our prophetic destinies by hearing God more clearly. It calls on us to make changes or to alter—or as the Schatzlines put it, to "altar"—our prayer lifestyles so as to push back the strongholds of darkness in our families, our churches, the marketplace, and ultimately our nations. If you are seeking to return or restore your place in God's holy priesthood for prayer, reading this book is a step in right direction.

—Rev. Yang Tuck Yoong
Senior Pastor
Cornerstone Community Church, Singapore
Director, Bible College of Wales, Swansea

Now more than ever we must be an awakened church who understands the necessity of living a life surrendered at the altar of the Lord. In order to be awakened, we must be surrendered. It is only by coming to the altar of Jesus that a life of holiness and passion can be realized. *Rebuilding the Altar* is a must-read for every person who is hungering and thirsting after encounters that will bring life-changing, Spirit-filled revival and transformation. Thank

You, Lord, for bringing this now message to the body of Christ through my dear friends Pat and Karen Schatzline.

—REBECCA GREENWOOD
COFOUNDER, CHRISTIAN HARVEST INTERNATIONAL AND
STRATEGIC PRAYER ACTION NETWORK
FALCON, COLORADO

This book is dedicated to the warriors in the trenches who still believe this generation is worthy of an altar experience. These are those who have ignored the approval of man, the secularism of today's gospel, and the plaudits of the crowd, and have decided to restore the capital S to the Spirit and apply the little s to self. Together we will rebuild the altars and watch all those who are fervently hungry for a "deep calls to deep" encounter to finally make an appointment with their Savior.

CONTENTS

FOREWORD

O H, HOW I remember my upbringing in my home church. The services were mighty. Our pastor, my mentor, was a very prolific and anointed preacher. He lived such a godly life. I was around him for many years, almost every day, and I used to wonder if he was an angel or a human being. His life and integrity were a model for me as an impressionable young preacher. After his very powerful and moving messages he would then open the altars. Those altar services are imprinted in my spiritual DNA. The altar was where the messages became reality.

In my mind I can still see the precious faces of the saints God used to help pray us through to the baptism of the Holy Ghost. They prayed with sinners for salvation and a myriad of other concerns that God's people brought to the altar. I remember Brother Alvin Locke, Brother Junior Kirkland, Sister Seagers, Sister Bramblett, Sister McClendon, Sister Riley, and so many others who are all in glory now. They had such an anointing to help people break through to victory. I can still hear the haunting sounds of those breakthrough moments. There were shrieks of joy, shouts of praise, sounds of victory, and lots of tears. I really wonder how many pastors and churches still maintain the altars in our houses of worship today. It indeed is the need of the hour.

As I began to write this foreword, it became increasingly clear to me that one of the reasons our nation is in the condition it is in is because many of the pulpits and pews have sanitized the church of the power and gifts of the Holy Spirit. Many have become ashamed and uncomfortable, even afraid of any demonstration of the power of God. I have the conviction that many church attenders leave church every week not dissatisfied but unsatisfied. They love their church, their pastor, and the people, but they leave empty and hungry for something they did not receive. They leave unsatisfied.

Pat and Karen are my spiritual son and daughter. There is no doubt that this new book is what is on God's mind. It has the breath of God on every page. I love the spirit in which they deal with delicate matters without compromise. I love how they write with anointed authority.

When I started to read the manuscript, I was wondering if this would be just another perspective on the need to return to the altar or a quick-fix book. However, I realized in the first few pages that it was a rare combination of a clear commitment to the Word of God and keen insight into where the body of Christ is at this moment concerning the conditions with which people really struggle and where their help can be found. People are yearning for what many of us experienced when we grew up in church, which is altar time.

This is no academic treatise. It is filled with insight, not suggestion. It is a clarion call to return and rebuild the altar. I wish this book had been available to put into the hands of many ministers and hungry parishioners long ago. Anointing flows from every page. Revelation comes from the teaching and preaching of the Word of God, but the reality comes at the altar.

—JOHN KILPATRICK
FOUNDER AND LEAD PASTOR
CHURCH OF HIS PRESENCE
DAPHNE, ALABAMA

FOREWORD

I T's TIME FOR the altar call. Having grown up in the home of a revivalist, I learned at a very young age that one of the most important parts of the revival meeting was the altar call. Yet the whole of our lives should be about living on the altar. As you open the pages of this book, listen to the cry of the Spirit as He describes His altar and the fire that burns upon it. Pat and Karen will bring you to the altar, where the God who answers by fire will answer you. At this altar Christ Jesus is encountered, sin is removed by His blood, and the fire of God consumes the sacrifice with the glory and power of His presence.

Today we have the opportunity to receive the same fire that fell on the Day of Pentecost, but the sacrifice must be ready. The sacrifice the Lord requires was revealed in Christ Jesus. Now, through the gift of salvation, His life has been imparted to us that we might be conformed to His image. Created anew in Him, our lives are to be as a whole burnt offering on the altar of God. We are no longer living to ourselves.

The sacrifice made holy and acceptable by the precious blood of Jesus is God's purchased possession. It is this kind of living sacrifice that God demands, and when it is made ready, the fire of His presence will fall. When our only desire is to be engulfed with the life of the Lord, the words of Evan Roberts will ring true: "I have built the altar, and laid the wood in order, and have prepared the offering; I have only to wait for the fire."[1]

God has sanctified the altar where we worship. He has shown us how we are to approach Him. The fire of God will not fall upon the altars fashioned by men. It will not consume the earthly offerings produced by the arm of flesh. God will be sanctified in those who approach Him. His presence is holy, His altar is holy, and the sacrifice must be holy too. The God who answers by fire will consume the offering that He has prepared; anything else is unacceptable. The altar has been built. Is the sacrifice of your life ready to live in the fire of His glory? It is God's desire to baptize you every day in the fire of His presence.

—Dr. Mark Spitsbergen
Pastor, Abiding Place
San Diego, California

OUR PRAYER FOR YOU

DEAR READER,

We pray the following prayer for all who dare to embark on a journey to be "altared" and undone at the altar of transformation.

As you begin to read the pages of this book, we pray that you will be awakened to your purpose and your destiny. We pray that there will begin to burn inside you a fire that cannot be extinguished and a hunger and thirst for more than what you have settled for that can only be satisfied in the presence of a living, loving, and powerful Savior. We pray that you will be drawn into a deeper encounter with God than you have ever experienced, and that in His presence you will find joy beyond flesh, fulfillment beyond position, and prestige and freedom in your surrender. May you abandon lethargy, complacency, and compromise as you realize there is a place where you can be consumed and set ablaze for something bigger than yourself.

We pray that you will find the courage to go beyond comfort, laying aside fear and stepping into the "God adventure" that awaits you when you decide that the task of rebuilding the altar in your life is worth coming to the end of yourself so you can see beyond the natural and into the very heart and presence of God. We pray that by the time you come to the end of this book you will find yourself lying before the very presence of God changed forever and armed with your purpose so that generations to come will be "altared" by your willingness to journey where others refused to go. God awaits you at the altar. If you build the altar, God will provide the fire, and the masses will come to watch it burn.

Let us become "the fellowship of the altared"!

—PAT AND KAREN

CALLING THE ALTARED!

THE MONUMENTAL JOURNEY of writing this book began late one night roughly twenty years ago following a discussion about the altar. In May 1997 we were youth pastors at Calvary Assembly of God in Decatur, Alabama. The church and the youth ministry were in a state of revival. Brownsville Assembly of God, which was just a four-hour drive south of us in Pensacola, Florida, was also experiencing the winds of revival. Our senior pastors, George and Phyllis Sawyer, were desperate for more of God, and this passion had taken hold of the church staff as well.

We were young pastors at the time, and we were zealous to see God pour out His Spirit in north Alabama. Secretly, though, something was stirring within us. We realized later that God was getting ready to move us to the next level, and part of His process was to create this stirring in our spirits. What used to satisfy our spirit just wasn't working anymore.

I (Pat) remember praying early one morning in the living room of our small condo. As I lay there, I suddenly saw a vision of King David carrying the ark of the covenant back to Israel. I said, "Lord, why am I seeing this?" He replied, "Son, I am asking you and Karen to carry My mercy seat back to America." I knew in that moment that God was calling us to be evangelists. In fact, until 2015 our ministry was called Mercy Seat Ministries. We changed the name to Remnant Ministries International in 2015 after a new revelation came to us.

As I lay on the floor praying that morning, our son, who was five at the time, came and lay on the floor beside me. "Daddy," he said, "why do you cry all the time?" I smiled at him and replied, "Because Daddy hurts for this generation." Suddenly the Lord spoke to me again. He said, "Son, you weep because you are mourning your own death."

"Lord," I replied, "what do You mean?"

"What I mean is this," God replied. "If I am going to use you and Karen, you must die to everything. You must build Me an altar."

Together we have traveled more than two million miles to the four corners of the earth. We have seen hundreds of thousands saved, renewed, filled with the Spirit, and healed. It has not been easy, but we have been kept by God's presence, which we experience only by being obedient to meet Him at the altar.

We are known for giving altar calls at our meetings, and we have seen thousands touched and transformed at the altar. Yet many have abandoned that place of surrender and obedience. The altars of our churches have become the steps by which man ascends the platform rather than the place to learn to walk in God's steps! Sadly we now live in a day when God would be treated as a stranger if He were to show up in many of our churches.

If we are to experience the transformative power of God, we must return to the altar. When Jesus stretched out His arms on the cross, He was telling mankind, "Now you can have access to meet with God!" Jesus's entire ministry on earth was established so that we could have direct access to heaven. The altar is so much more than a wooden or marble piece of furniture that we visit to dedicate a child, get married, or hold a funeral. Because of Jesus the altar is a lifestyle of devotion and renewal in God's presence. As Peter wrote, "To this you were called, because Christ suffered for you, leaving you an example, that you should follow in his steps" (1 Pet. 2:21).

A CRY FOR MORE

Years after God wrecked us in May 1997, we had another similar experience. We again realized that what we were doing was no longer working. In our spirits there was a cry for more, but we didn't quite understand the deep feeling of discontent that we were experiencing in ministry. We had no reason to feel this way; we were very happy with our lives. We were living the dream of the "called." Doors were wide open to our ministry to go out and be heard. We had "arrived," yet we were feeling the sting of spiritual frustration.

We began to question if this was all there was for us. We had seen some glorious outpourings of God in our meetings, and the Lord had always provided for us when needs arose. God had allowed us to travel over a million miles on four different continents preaching the gospel. We had seen tens of thousands saved, miracle after miracle take place, and thousands running to the altar to encounter the

Savior, which is the greatest sight on earth. Nevertheless, we found ourselves desperate for something even greater.

The longing we felt was not for more platforms, plaudits, platitudes, or even promotion. It was Jesus knocking at the door of our hearts. We soon realized that it was a Psalm 42:7 "deep calling unto deep" season for us. The One who had created us longed to know us in a deeper way. We had grown stagnant spiritually, and we were becoming distant from the One we had called Father for so long.

God in His mercy was actually rescuing us, asking us to preach a message most of the satisfied saints would not receive and postmodern hipster theologians would consider cannon fodder. This longing in our spirits, this discontent, this cry for more forced us to awaken to the prophetic, particularly the areas of dreams, and to signs and wonders. God was taking us deeper than we had ever gone before, but it was painful!

The combination of frustration and agitation was God's way of whispering and, at times, even shouting that there is more beyond where we had pitched our spiritual tent. My friend Paul Owens once said, "Frustration and agitation are the mother of intercession."[1] Solomon said it best in Ecclesiastes 7:3: "Frustration is better than laughter, because a sad face is good for the heart." God will frustrate you to get you to move past where you have camped out. You were not called to sit and do nothing.

In our personal frustration we came to the crossroads of dissatisfaction and destiny. Paul said it well when he wrote, "For the creation was subjected to frustration, not by its own choice, but by the will of the one who subjected it, in hope that the creation itself will be liberated from its bondage to decay and brought into the freedom and glory of the children of God" (Rom. 8:20–21). In other words, God loved us so much that He refused to allow us to be comfortable with the life we were living.

It is an age-old rule for the called of God—just when you find that you are satisfied, God will create a scenario to make sure you are not also becoming complacent, because a God adventure is the only thing that will satisfy those we like to call "the wanderers of holy ground"! Paul wrote of the process of transformation when he said, "But we all, with unveiled face, beholding as in a mirror the glory of the Lord, are being transformed into the same image from glory to glory, just as from the Lord, the Spirit" (2 Cor. 3:18, NASB). We have learned that many times in order to go from glory to glory, one must cross bridges of adversity between each glory. On the journey across the bridge your comfort zone can become a very uncomfortable place.

Do not read this book if you are satisfied with a life of spiritual mediocrity, which will, in turn, cause God to simply be a stranger when you arrive to meet Him in heaven. God's call requires a response as it takes you on an adventure in faith, freedom, authority, wisdom, blessing, spiritual identity, and dying to self. Although we will discuss the physical church altar, this call of God is about a personal and deep encounter with the One who hung between the thieves. It is at the altar of the cross that we once again desire to see God more than we desire people, platforms, or plaudits; where we become plaintiffs in the courts of heaven and not defendants in the inner circle of the religious!

This is not a call for the satisfied or those who recoil

at the thought of God invading their space. It is a call to hungry hearts, a call to the realization that the ultimate altar was a cross that held the jewel of heaven (Heb. 10:12–13). Are you willing to run, walk, or even crawl back to the place where your freedom awaits, to lay aside the day-to-day, nonstop busyness and dust off the altar of encounter? If so, then you might just be a prime candidate to become what we call "the altared"—those who have realized that without a daily encounter with God, life will never be complete. The altared have experienced Psalm 32:7, and that is their cry: "You are my hiding place."

Do You Dare Continue Like This?

God has a challenge for you, and it begins with the question, "Dare you continue like this?" The answer will awaken you to a whole new world. Our vision for this book is that it will leave you with a hunger to go deeper and a desire to create change. Those who are hungry for more of God will feast upon this message. However, those who are satisfied with self will determine early on that this challenge should be relegated to yesterday's expression of church or viewed as an irrelevant message that is best kept under wraps lest it upset the status quo.

God wants to use each of us to change the world. There is a line forming that begins on the day you were born and ends the day you die. We call this "the dash." It is time to be accountable for your dash, to make your dash count! We are called to be overcomers—no more licking the wounds of past pain and rejection. It is time to step into your destiny. Will you be known as God's representative of freedom, willing to be used to change the future?

The hunger and cries of the redeemed must be brought to the altar of the cross. Your response to God will always determine the future of your family and those in your sphere of influence.

Many years ago I (Pat) had the honor of spending a couple days with one of our dear friends, Pastor Larry Stockstill. He had invited his son Joel, myself, and another minister to spend time at a camp with him. Pastor Larry believes strongly in discipling young ministers. Today many of the greatest leaders in our nation can say they once served under him. During that camp he began to share with us the importance of the altar call. He told us there are always four altar calls that must be given at the end of a service: one for the lost, one for those who have wandered away from God and need a fresh encounter with Him, one for those who are weary or sick, and one for those who want to stay on fire. We have endeavored to always remember those four groups in every altar call we have given. Our hope is that this book touches all four groups.

Are you ready to be altared? It may cost you man's approval, but it will open new realms of freedom. The call to be "the altared" is not for the celebrities looking only to impress the church paparazzi and build their personal social media accounts with 140 characters of self-gratification, amplified grace, and irrelevant grand-standing. No! The media coverage of "the altared" should always be an obituary of self and a birth announcement of the spirit of revival! If you accept the challenge to be "altared," then your journey begins here, where "even the sparrow has found a home, and the swallow a nest for herself, where she may have her young—a place near your altar, LORD Almighty, my King and my God" (Ps. 84:3).

Maybe, just maybe, as you run to the altar, you too will experience what the prophet Isaiah felt when he wrote:

> At the sound of their voices the doorposts and thresholds shook and the temple was filled with smoke. "Woe to me," I cried. "I am ruined! For I am a man of unclean lips, and I live among a people of unclean lips, and my eyes have seen the King, the LORD Almighty." Then one of the seraphim flew to me with a live coal in his hand, which he had taken with tongs from the altar. With it he touched my mouth and said, "See, this has touched your lips; your guilt is taken away and your sin atoned for." Then I heard the voice of the Lord saying, "Whom shall I send? And who will go for us?" And I said, "Here am I. Send me!"
>
> —ISAIAH 6:4–8

It is with great excitement that we share our life message with you. We believe that every single page of this book will stir your heart for more of Jesus, reminding you afresh that the knock at the door of your spirit is not another opportunity to exalt self. Rather, it is the knock of a victorious Savior calling you deeper in Him! God is waiting for you to dust off the altars of encounter and enter the most holy place. Allow Him to prepare you to be stirred, challenged, and strengthened. This is a clarion call for "the altared" to climb once again upon a forgotten place where our Savior continually calls out, "Come to Me" (Matt. 11:28, MEV).

THE DECLARATION OF THE ALTARED

We are "the altared"! We are those who will no longer squander the daylight with things that do not matter. We live to climb upon the altar, encounter the power and presence of God, and allow His light to shine brightly through us to a lost and dying world!

CHAPTER 1

MEET ME AT THE ALTAR!

I (PAT) WAS SIXTEEN years old when God walked into my bedroom late one night and radically changed me. I was far from having any kind of real relationship with God at the time; I was carousing with the wrong crowd and generally making a mess of my life. Being a "PK," a pastor's kid, I had seen both the good and bad side of ministry up close and personal and didn't want any part of it. My precious mom's health had suffered from the pressures of ministry life. Although God would heal her and eventually restore our family in a powerful way, I couldn't see past my anger at the time. In the midst of acting out I found myself at a crossroads, with a deep cry in my heart for an authentic and personal relationship with God. No matter how hard I tried, there seemed to be no way to quiet the longing in my heart. My parents' revelation of God wasn't working for me. I needed my own God encounter. As I lay there that night unable to sleep, I cried out, "God, if You are real, I need to know it. Otherwise I'm done with Christianity."

I crawled out of bed and lay on the floor as I'd seen my father do when he would pray. I had never done anything like that before, but in my desperation I was willing to try anything. Lying there on the floor in my little basement bedroom in our house in Oneonta, Alabama, wanting God and wondering if He would visit me, I began to pray. Nothing happened, and after a while I started to doze off when suddenly He showed up! I could feel His presence in the room. "God," I cried out. "If You're real, speak to me! I need to hear You speak to me!"

It was a heart cry and God answered. "Pat," He said, "I love you, and I have a plan for your life." Then He continued. "I am sorry you have seen things in My church that have hurt you, but if you will follow Me, I will use you to heal people." God's words to me that night transformed my life. My life didn't turn around completely that night. God had more work to do in me. But because He revealed Himself to me in that altar moment, I was able to take the first halting steps back to restoration.

Are you longing for that place of encounter with God that will change everything? A place where one can come empty but leave with more than can ever be imagined? A place of surrender that leads to a life of captivating moments, where you experience freedom while anchored to something bigger than yourself? A place where joy is matched by desperation and authority is matched by surrender, where you encounter the greatest love and leave with the never-ending realization that there is more? A place where you receive grace for the past and grace for the future?

Though many have abandoned this place, most still long to find it. It is not geographically prejudicial. It can be found in a bedroom, a church, jail, car, nursery, hospital, asylum, mansion, shack, office, sports arena, refugee camp, boat, strip club, cabin, or penthouse! In fact, it's right in front of you. It has always been there; you can't avoid it. It calls to you. It is a place just past the pain, the embarrassment, and the hurt; it's past all these things but right before your future. And it has always been there—the "altar" has always been right in front of you.

When I was growing up in church, no one ever explained the altar. There was an expectation that we would go to the altar, but we never quite understood why. Over time it became evident that the altar was a place where one could get real about life. Yet it felt awkward at times to walk down to the church altar. Sometimes it seemed like going to the altar was a way of publicly showing others that one wasn't such a bad person, almost like appearing before a parole board. It would have been better if someone had explained the purpose of the altar, but perhaps no one did because no one really understood what the altar is.

The altar is a special place that holds some of life's greatest breakthroughs. It is not just a physical place but rather a lifestyle. In our walk with God we must eventually come to a place where we are eager to encounter God at the altar, for that is where freedom awaits. And it is where transformation begins. The altar is where who you have been gets interrupted by who you can become.

The altar I speak of is alive. It has always called to you, and there you will find answers to all your questions. But be warned—you will have to battle self when you arrive at the altar. Yet once you climb upon it, once you grab hold of it, once you experience it, self will leave, flesh will die, and your spirit will live once again. This is what the altar is all about. Oswald Chambers once said, "Leave the broken, irreversible past in God's hands, and step out into the invincible future with Him."[1] Are you ready for God's invincible future?

Our dear friend Dr. Rodney Howard-Browne, who is a powerful voice in our life, called us one day as we were writing about the altar and gave us a powerful word from the Lord. He told us that leaders in the body of Christ must introduce people to God "and arrange the meeting.... And if they are desperate, they shall experience the move of God like no one has ever seen."[2]

I am reminded of the night God visited me with that very message. It was October 6, 2013. I had just finished ministering in a church in Blytheville, Arkansas. When I am on the road, I have a nightly ritual that helps anchor me to the things of God. Just before falling asleep I pray, "O Lord, I want to see You in my sleep, so please visit me tonight." Karen and I both do this when we travel. We like to joke and say we have a sleep disorder called revelation because when we ask Him, God speaks to us in prophetic dreams.

As I crawled into bed in my hotel room that night, I uttered my "Please visit me tonight, God" prayer and then fell asleep. Around about 1:30 a.m. I was suddenly awakened by an overwhelming fear of the Lord. The room was full of His glory. God was visiting me! I was having an altar encounter in my hotel room! His presence was so intense that I found myself crying out, "Lord, please do not come any closer or I will die!" I even repented for asking to see Him. Then He spoke. "Pat," He said. "If you will give Me everything, I will give you everything. You must tell this generation that if they give Me everything, I will give them abundant life." Then, as suddenly as He had appeared, He was gone. I was left weeping and transformed, endued with boldness and passion as never before by this intimate encounter.

THE FIRST ALTAR

The entire Bible is predicated on one thing—that God desires to know us in an intimate, real, and powerful way. That means when we draw near to meet with God, He will draw near to us (James 4:8). The Old Testament began with God's creating His masterpiece called mankind, only to have this amazing love affair with humanity interrupted by a liar named Satan (Gen. 3:4). Eventually humanity would become so deceived and perverted that God would regret that He made them (Gen. 6:7). It was then that God decided it was time to start over. There was only one man left who had found favor with God. Genesis 6:9 says, "Noah was a righteous man, blameless among the people of his time, and he walked faithfully with God." It was this man whom God told to build an ark (v. 14).

Noah worked on this boat for 120 years. This was a massive boat measuring 450 feet long, 75 feet wide, and 45 feet high.[3] Can you imagine? Everyone laughed at him; he looked like a lunatic. Imagine people coming from far and wide to see this thing called a boat. You must remember that until this point, water had come up from the ground but never from the sky. The people laughed—until it began to rain (Gen. 7:10). This rain was the beginning of a massive flood God sent to wipe out every inhabitant on earth except Noah, his family, and the animals on the ark (v. 23). After 150 days the rain stopped and the water began to recede, leaving the ark resting upon Mount Ararat.

When Noah and his family exited the ark, the first thing Noah did was to build an altar—the first altar.

> Then Noah built an altar to the LORD and took of every clean animal and of every clean bird and offered burnt offerings on the altar. The LORD smelled a soothing aroma; and the LORD said in His heart, "I will never again curse the ground because of man, for the inclination of man's heart is evil from his youth, nor will I again destroy every living thing as I have done."
> —GENESIS 8:20–21, MEV

The altar caused God to draw near, softening His heart. Think of it—the altar changed man's relationship with our mighty God. Death brought redemption through an altar! Why is this important? It is important because this altar began man's journey toward redemption. God would use this magnificent centerpiece of the entire Old Testament as a way for man to move toward redemption. If there is one word that best describes the entire Bible, it is redemption.

With God and His creation separated, God required a sacrificial offering to bring us close again. It is significant that, even as far back as Noah's day, without sacrifice man could not truly have a relationship with God. The altar has always been the place God has used to bring life out of death. This is why when Jesus was trying to get His disciples to understand His purpose on earth, He said, "Truly, truly I say to you, unless a grain of wheat falls into the ground and dies, it remains alone. But if it dies, it bears much fruit" (John 12:24, MEV). Without redemption you and I would be doomed to an eternity absent from the love of God. The altar is used from this point on in Scripture as the place of sacrifice and freedom.

God gave guidelines as to how the altar was to be used. He told Israel the type of sacrifices that were to go on the altar and how to build a proper altar. According to the website Bible History Online, "God said that without the shedding of blood there would be no remission of sins. The blood sacrifice was the life of the innocent victim receiving death so that the one offering could go free. The sacrificial offering was a substitutionary atonement, the innocent victim would receive the full weight of God's judgment, while the guilty person making the sacrifice would receive forgiveness and justification and atonement from God. The sacrifice literally became sin, and therefore was called a sin offering."[4]

The altar became the place where people could finally get free from their burdens. And that hasn't changed. The altar is the rallying place that transforms our mistakes into God's victory! And it is the place where God's priests must live (Joel 1:13).

The problem was that man needed an ultimate sacrifice. The Bible says the blood of animals couldn't keep covering our sin (Heb. 10:4–5). There had to be an ultimate sacrifice. Man needed a lamb, a Savior who would save the world from the sins of humankind. Man needed someone to do away with the old and establish a new life (Heb. 10:9).

The Lamb is named Jesus! For thousands of years humanity waited for a Savior. Finally He arrived! It was the ultimate altar call the night He was born. Yet the final altar had to be built before the Savior could be placed there. Many prophets foretold that a Messiah would come and rescue man. It is written in Job 19:25, "For I know that my Redeemer lives, and He will stand at last on the earth" (MEV). The word translated *Redeemer* in this verse, or *ga'al* in the Hebrew, means the avenger or to ransom or redeem by payment.[5]

The prophet Isaiah gave us the best clues that Jesus is this Redeemer:

> Therefore the Lord Himself shall give you a sign: The virgin shall conceive, and bear a son, and shall call his name Immanuel.
>
> —ISAIAH 7:14, MEV

> For unto us a child is born, unto us a son is given, and the government shall be upon his shoulder. And his name shall be called Wonderful Counselor, Mighty God, Eternal Father, Prince of Peace.
>
> —ISAIAH 9:6, MEV

> He was oppressed, and he was afflicted, yet he opened not his mouth; he was brought as a lamb to the slaughter, and as a sheep before its shearers is silent, so he opened not his mouth.
>
> —ISAIAH 53:7, MEV

THE CHRISTMAS ALTAR CALL

Can you imagine what it must have been like for the shepherds who were keeping watch on that seemingly ordinary night on a hillside near Bethlehem? Just as they were settling in for an uneventful night, suddenly their senses were overwhelmed with an explosion in the sky. God was announcing the birth of His son with a brilliant star in the night sky, and He was about to give the first altar call to bow to Jesus. He was putting forth an invitation to welcome the King of the world! The King of kings would be born in humble surroundings, among animals, sewage, the harsh elements of nature, and a world in need of redemption. Is this not the way God always brings greatness— from the foundation of humility?

It is in the hibernation of holiness that real fruit is produced, not on the stage. God began His everlasting work in a manger, which was little more than a cave. Yet this little King would let out a cry from His tiny lungs that would cause creation to sit up and say, "He has arrived!" As the shepherds stood watch, suddenly the angel of the Lord declared, "Do not be afraid. I bring you good news that will cause great joy for all the people. Today in the town of David a Savior has been born to you; he is the Messiah, the Lord. This will be a sign to you: You will find a baby wrapped in cloths and lying in a manger." The Bible then says, "Suddenly a great company of the heavenly host appeared with the angel, praising God and saying, 'Glory to God in the highest heaven, and on earth peace to those on whom his favor rests'" (Luke 2:10–14).

Jesus had come to rescue mankind from the lies and grip of Satan! This awakening of the shepherds in the night would lead them to a Lamb who would eventually be led to the slaughter. The humble awakening in their hearts would lead them to the salvation purchased on a cross. Humanity would come know how much God loved the world through the sacrifice of His Son. Old Testament prophecy would finally be fulfilled.[6] God used 23,145 verses comprising the thirty-nine books in the Old

Testament[7] to lead to the crescendo of angels giving the first altar call after the birth of Jesus. It was the ultimate "O come, all ye faithful" moment in which man first experienced the "on bended knee I come" transformation.

Christmas is about the beginning of all that we hold dear! Without the birth of the Christ child the veil that kept us from relationship with God would never have been torn. Mankind's restoration lay in a shanty, a lean-to, a feeding trough, so that mankind could become temples of the Holy Ghost! Because Christ was born in that manger, favor could rest on the meek and lowly. Hallelujah to the Lamb! This first altar call was not an interruption of a well-produced one-hour-and-ten-minute service that would not scare off the seeker, but rather a place where the seeker could find hope, restoration, and freedom. This first altar call would alter all of humanity! There were no naysayers, scoffers, mockers, or religious zealots invited so they could use their "hipster" theology to explain away the divinity. No, there were only humble, dirty men who were awakened by messengers of light!

This encounter should awaken us all to the fact that no matter how many times we have fallen away, been wounded, or left without hope, God has made a way for our salvation in Jesus. The angels allowed their worship to spill over into the earth's atmosphere that glorious night.

- This opening of the sky would lead to the rending of a veil (Matt. 27:51).

- This child wrapped in swaddling clothes would one day stand naked before mankind (Matt. 27:28–30) and set the world ablaze.

- The cry of a baby Lamb would someday lead to the roar of a mighty Lion (Luke 23:13–47; Rev. 5:5).

- This innocent little gift from heaven would become the doorway to God (Heb. 10:20)!

The Son of God put down His glory so that mankind could experience Him in their hearts.

Thirty years from that night in the stable in Bethlehem Jesus began His earthly ministry. John the Baptist announced it, declaring "Behold! The Lamb of God who takes away the sin of the world!" (John 1:29, NKJV). Jesus would perform miracle after miracle. He healed the sick, cast out demons, showed compassion, loved the oppressed, gave hope, fed the hungry, and cursed the religious. The Bible says He accomplished so much while He walked the earth that the whole world would not have room for the books that could be written to share all that He had done (John 21:25).

However, that was not why He came. Mankind had a Lamb, but we still needed an altar. Jesus was to be our sacrificial Lamb, yet when the time came, everyone in His inner circle tried to stop Him. The disciples wanted to crown Him as their earthly king, but Jesus understood He would be glorified according to God's plan. There is a big difference between God's plans and the plans of men. When it came time for Jesus to be our Lamb, He faced the greatest trial in human history. Yet because of Jesus's journey of pain, man was able to walk the aisle to the altar!

This must not be treated flippantly as simply a religious act or a pious experience from a bygone church era.

Because of the altar, mankind now has access to the throne of God! Jesus made eight stops on His way to the altar. These eight stops are often referred to as the Stations of the Cross. It is these eight stations that lead to your altar:

- Station 1: Pilate condemns Jesus to die (Matt. 27:26).
- Station 2: Jesus accepts His cross (John 19:17).
- Station 3: Simon helps carry the cross (Luke 23:26).
- Station 4: Jesus speaks to the women (Luke 23:28).
- Station 5: Jesus is stripped of His garments (John 19:23).
- Station 6: Jesus is nailed to the cross (Matt. 27:3–56; Phil. 2:8).
- Station 7: Jesus cares for His mother (John 19:26).
- Station 8: Jesus dies on the cross (Luke 23:44–46; 1 Pet. 2:24).

The altar was expensive! It bankrupted the heavens for you and me. What began as a selfish act under a tree in a garden would lead to a selfless act upon a tree on a hill. For three days all of creation waited. Galatians 3:13 says, "But Christ has rescued us from the curse pronounced by the law. When he was hung on the cross, he took upon himself the curse for our wrongdoing. For it is written in the Scriptures, 'Cursed is everyone who is hung on a tree'" (NLT). The cross became the ultimate altar—the place by which man would have access to life through the perfect sin offering who laid down His life for His wandering bride.

Then Jesus arose! He conquered death, hell, and the grave; the Lamb saved mankind. The Bible also says in Hebrews 13:10, "We have an altar from which those who minister at the tabernacle have no right to eat." Don't you see? Christ is our altar. Jesus became the sin offering so that you and I could experience freedom. Now we have the ability to change our family tree.

The church is too often the place where doughnuts and coffee are more important than what the lowly shepherds were commanded to do. We must rebuild the altar! Leaders who render the altar encounter a lost cause desire community over communion. The church must desire to see God once again! The body of Christ can restore the altar so that all of humanity can hear, "Come to me, all you who are weary and burdened, and I will give you rest. Take my yoke upon you and learn from me, for I am gentle and humble in heart, and you will find rest for your souls. For my yoke is easy and my burden is light" (Matt. 11:28–30).

We have progressed from the flood to the river! Noah put a door on the ark through which he could save his family (Gen. 6:16), and he would use the wood from those doors to build the first altar! Jesus became the door for us to escape the curse of sin (John 14:6); Jesus's body opened wide the door (Heb. 10:20). The first altar started after a horrible flood, and the greatest altar ends with a river, as John 7:38 says: "He who believes in Me, as the Scripture has said, out of his heart shall flow rivers of living water" (MEV).

The altar is open, and no one stands in the way. Do not allow man, fear, religion, or minions to keep you from the place the shepherds once beheld. Hebrews 4:16 says, "Let us then approach God's throne of grace with confidence, so that we may receive mercy and find grace to help us in our time of need."

Dr. Grant McClung, president of Missions Resource Group, wrote an excellent article titled "We Have an Altar (Hebrews 13:10)."[8] In it he outlines five aspects of an altar experience. The first is confession and forgiveness of sin. When we confess with our mouth that "Jesus is Lord," we are forgiven and cleansed of all unrighteousness (1 John 1:8–9). Second, when we come to the altar of prayer, the old falls away as the new comes (2 Cor. 5:17). With Christ in us, we are transformed into His new creation.

Third, the altar is the place for each one of us to encounter the living God. As we draw close to Him, God draws near to us (James 4:7–8), and in His presence we are washed clean and consecrated for His service (Heb. 10:19–22). Fourth, it is at the altar that we join with the community that is the body of Christ in the great communion of the saints so that together we may encourage and exhort one another (Heb. 10:23–25). And fifth, at the altar we receive our commissioning for ministry just as Isaiah, Ananias, Saul, and others did.

As Dr. McClung wrote, "May we never forget, and never fail to impart to the next generation, that 'we have an altar'—that special place and experience with God where we experience Confession (and forgiveness) of our sins, transformational Change, a special Consecration/closeness to God, the Communion of the saints, and our purpose for living in His Commission in to the world."[9]

These five steps are key in the life of every believer. Are you ready to put one foot in front of the other and begin the walk down the road to the altar? If so, read on!

Chapter 2

WHERE HAVE THE ALTARS GONE?

It's always exciting to see churches on the cutting edge of technology, ones structurally organized for growth and doing everything they can to make their houses user friendly. This is refreshing because it shows God is presented in the most excellent way. From the parking lot to the reserved seating for guests, all the checkpoints of welcome are marked off. The proof is in the growth—from multiple services to multiple sites. Many of these churches definitely have what you could call the "relevant factor"!

But are they changing the world? People are coming, so God must be pleased, right? Offering plates are full, so God must be pleased, right? The messages are catchy and visual, so God must be pleased, right? Looking deeper, you sometimes find conviction is no longer encouraged because the cross took care of that, right? You learn that grace is no longer preached as an invitation to transformation. Churches rarely speak of Holy Spirit fire these days because they fear the masses don't like their services to become unpredictable. We are, after all, living in a day when services are on a timer and altar calls are for those who haven't figured Christianity out yet. It's amazing that we have come so far in our ability to "do church" that we no longer remember *we are the church*!

Given all this, we can't help but wonder if being relevant is simply a way to fire the Holy Spirit from His job so things will never get messy. That's much easier than deliverance—because deliverance is never easy, and true discipleship is more than a six-week journey. In a day of celebrity-driven ministry where a nonconfrontational message of hope wants to rule the day, church often becomes an empty experience and not an encounter with God.

I (Pat) remember well a particularly messy altar moment in February of 1995. I was in Phoenix, Arizona, with our church staff to attend Tommy Barnett's pastors' school along with about ten thousand other pastors. This was a five-day event. The youth ministry Karen and I led was becoming well-known. Yet while our ministry to youth was expanding, our personal priorities were seriously out of whack. During one of the evening services the school held its graduation for its Master's Commission program, which sent young leaders to serve in their communities to get a firsthand understanding of people's physical and spiritual needs.

The place was packed and testimonies abounded from the graduates of how their lives had been transformed by seeing the love and power of Jesus in action. At one point a young man named Jay Bakker stood up and began to share his story. Many did not realize that he was the son of evangelist Jim Bakker, who had gone to prison several years earlier in a scandal that had shut down the PTL Club and Heritage USA. As Jay finished sharing his story of redemption and deep pain, Pastor Barnett announced that there was someone very special in the building. Suddenly down the aisle came Jim Bakker, broken and humbled. The room erupted in a standing ovation. Jim would later tell Karen and me that was the scariest moment of his life. He was expecting the pastors to jeer him and hurl insults, but instead he was met with a standing ovation that must have lasted ten minutes. It was a beautiful picture of redemption.

As he took the stage beside his son, Jim asked forgiveness of the ministers and his son, and then he began sharing stories. One story in particular hit us hard. While he was in prison, people had sent him pictures they had taken during the time he was building Heritage USA. In many of the pictures there was his young son, following behind him. He confessed right there to his son Jay that in his own busyness he never realized that Jay was there, right behind him. Then he told us that Jay had spent his sixteenth birthday visiting him in prison. When Jim apologized publicly to his son, Jay replied, "Dad, I had waited my whole life to spend one uninterrupted day with you. That birthday was the best day of my life."

There was not a dry eye in the building. Pastors were weeping because we too had put ministry over family so many times. That day was the beginning of Jim Bakker's restoration. He has since become a major influence in our life. His brokenness and desperation for God challenge us every time we are with him and his wife, Lori Graham Bakker. As the service came to a close, I ran out to the pay phones, as did a lot of other pastors, to call home and talk to our son, Nate, who was staying with friends back in Alabama. On the phone that night I promised Nate that I would always be a dad who was there for him, through thick and thin.

The messy confession of a very broken man brought about a supernatural transformation in many of our lives that night. It was an altar moment that would change me forever. Our son, Nate, is grown now and a father himself. I can honestly say that we are best friends because one man had the guts to walk down the aisle and get real. Those in the pews must see the brokenness that is produced by godly sorrow if they are to come to repentance. "Godly sorrow brings repentance that leads to salvation and leaves no regret, but worldly sorrow brings death" (2 Cor. 7:10).

I find it sad that so many leaders today are unwilling to lay life, limb, and reputation down for a move of God that brings repentance and centers around a message of holiness. God is looking for men and women who will exit stage left so the attention can rest on the overwhelming power of an auspicious God. The church will change once again as God raises up righteous voices of truth and when we no longer give audience to those who practice loose morals, regurgitate hyper-grace messages, and seek to beguile congregants with their personalities rather than flowing in the power of God's Word.

Truly the next generation of leaders God is raising up understands that the greatest challenge, the one that brings next-level anointing, is to let go of selfish ambition and popularity to carry a cross of humility and brokenness.

We must resist the seduction of man's Christianity, which so often causes us to abandon our confidence in the risen Savior and exchange it for a manufactured hope produced by a fallen man.

We have found ourselves living in a day when Christians are told to be quiet lest we offend someone and where "secular Christianity" is the new norm. The apostle Paul warned Timothy of these days, saying:

> Don't be naive. There are difficult times ahead. As the end approaches, people are going to be self-absorbed, money-hungry, self-promoting, stuck-up, profane, contemptuous of parents, crude, coarse, dog-eat-dog, unbending, slanderers, impulsively wild, savage, cynical, treacherous, ruthless, bloated windbags, addicted to lust, and allergic to God. They'll make a show of religion, but behind the scenes they're animals. Stay clear of these people.
> —2 TIMOTHY 3:1–5, THE MESSAGE

With all that's happening, our only recourse is to reinvent how we do church, right? We must make ourselves more relevant, right? Maybe the apostle Paul saw this day coming when he wrote, "Don't fool yourself. Don't think that you can be wise merely by being up-to-date with the times. Be God's fool—that's the path to true wisdom. What the world calls smart, God calls foolish. It's written in Scripture, He exposes the chicanery of the chic. The Master sees through the smoke screens of the know-it-alls" (1 Cor. 3:18–20, THE MESSAGE).

Why would any minister of the gospel rob this generation of a genuine encounter with God like the ones we had when we first began our journeys with Him? Could it be we are in a compassion crisis—that we love people's acceptance so much we aren't willing to tell them the truth that would rescue their souls? It's at the altar of redemption and not at the table of man's knowledge that we find freedom.

Are our churches built on popularity-driven platforms because it's easier for preachers to stand and declare who we are than to admit we have lost sight of who He is? Perhaps it's easier to say, "Look at me," because if we say, "Look at God," people may realize we don't look much like Him. So we reduce God down to "love" and "compassion" while ignoring holiness, righteousness, and mercy. Truly this should not be.

The altar call that once ended our services has been removed from the order of service to make room for fellowship. Many church leaders will be held in contempt in the court of the kingdom of God if they do not restore the holy meeting place to our gatherings. We have our weekly one-hour-and-ten-minute services that are noninvasive at their core and give us barely enough time to meet with God. Comfort is so important to the church experience today that we don't even hear God attempting to intrude on our schedules and parking problems over the espresso machines churning coffee beans. And this is the definition of church the visiting onlooker is being urged to be a part of today.

We have amazing slogans such as "a church for the imperfect" or "a place where you can be you." Now, mind you, there is nothing wrong with coffee or redefining church or outreach, but what is missing at the core of our gatherings is the infusion of the Word, the power of the

Holy Spirit, and the demonstration of signs and wonders. We have grown so accustomed to spectacular media presentations, timed talks, and eighties rock songs rehashed to be spiritual that it might harm the culture of our congregations if Jesus were to walk in and flip over the tables. This may seem harsh, but it is not meant to be. For those of you who grew up in staunch religious environments, the changes in church have been a breath of fresh air, but much of what we consider relevant has put the church in danger of becoming irrelevant.

One morning while praying, I heard the Holy Spirit say to me, "Pat, there's been a demonic onslaught sent from hell to make Christian leaders believe they must live like the world to win the world." The church's message is no longer clear that sin is sin and that God is "a rewarder of those who diligently seek Him" (Heb. 11:6, MEV).

Please understand: we believe understanding and love are critical to touching lives. After all, it is God's goodness that leads men to repentance (Rom. 2:4). But when do we give people a chance to repent? At the coffee bar? In a small group? On an encounter weekend that takes place three times a year? These are all good places to grow deep in God, but twice-a-month churchgoers must experience encounters when they actually come to church or they will be swept away by the lies of the enemy.

Has the dress of the bride become soiled with the filth of compromise? We must make a choice. If we aren't going to lead people to change, we may as well shut the church doors. We must not forget that Malachi 1:10 says, "'Oh, that one of you would shut the temple doors, so that you would not light useless fires on my altar! I am not pleased with you,' says the Lord Almighty, 'and I will accept no offering from your hands.'"[1]

It's Time for a Great Awakening

So many key prophetic voices around the world have told us they believe we are on the verge of a third great awakening. We too believe we are close to seeing a monumental spiritual shift in the land. We believe this coming awakening will arrest the hearts of men and women to once again believe that God must be first in our lives. With this awakening will surely come the greatest attack from Satan that has ever been released. The enemy "is filled with fury, because he knows that his time is short" (Rev. 12:12).

The attack from the enemy is not new. He will continue to subtly release toxic, perverted, mindless bile through the airwaves, the lecture podium, and the culture police who are hell-bent on stamping out anything to do with Christianity. This will lead to the rise of the Antichrist agenda and the Belial spirit spoken of in 2 Corinthians 6:14–15. The clouds of secular humanism, perversion, angst, and despair are hovering above our lives daily. And this attack is working because the bride of Christ is under the control of a terrorist called lethargy.

Lethargy creates an indention on the pew but will never put a dent in the devil's kingdom. The enemy has worn out the bride. Satan knows that a tired and exhausted bride will struggle to find her way to the altar of freedom. We are becoming much like Gideon's army, which was "faint, yet pursuing" (Judg. 8:4, kjv). As Daniel 7:25 says, "He [Satan] shall speak words against the Most High and shall wear out the saints of the Most High" (mev).

While the dust gathers, the church sleeps! What dust? The dust that gathers on the altar for lack of use. Have our altars become props for dramas while actors perform spiritual rituals to keep the masses happy? There was a time when the hurting went to church to get healed and delivered. This will not happen as long as we live in fear of man and ignore the onslaught of Satan. The systematic removal of God from the public square and the microwaving of church services that leaves little time for a Holy Spirit encounter, compounded with the cries of the righteous, have forced God's Spirit to wander in search of yielded vessels outside the church walls because those inside will not spend time at the altar of encounter. But the broken and contrite will enjoy daily tea with a mighty King. Those who render the altar encounter a lost cause are in direct correlation with those in the church who desire community with man over communion with God.

Throughout history heaven has invaded earth with a mandate from the Father for His people to rise up and lead. This seems to always happen when the church is asleep and the nation is imploding. It's as if God steps into our dimension and chooses to once again startle the compromised out of their slumber and release a fire in their hearts for more of Him. Our only hope is that God will interrupt our atmosphere, lest we be taken captive by the allure of a perverse culture. The stupefaction of an exhausted bride leads to the manifestation of cultural anarchy. Every day the righteous accept and even devour the enemy's agenda. A sleeping bride will always struggle with discernment because they are not awakened to the ways of God. The prophet Hosea said, "Whoever is wise, let him understand these things; whoever is discerning, let him know them. For the ways of the LORD are right, and the righteous will walk in them, but transgressors will stumble in them" (Hosea 14:9, NASB).

With the loss of the gift of discernment (1 Cor. 12:10) the church will begin to accept a culture that is in direct contradiction to God's plans. The nineteenth-century preacher Charles Spurgeon once said, "Discernment is not knowing the difference between right and wrong. It is knowing the difference between right and almost right."[2] How long before the cloud bursts and the flood consumes everyone? How long will we reject a sovereign God for the manufactured hope created by the systems of this world? Our nation, our churches, and our homes are at a crossroads. These are the days when a news alert interrupting your favorite television program is not so shocking anymore. It has become all too common to hear of demonstrations in the streets, terrorist attacks, wars and rumors of wars, famine and earthquakes, and the pervasiveness of perversion, yet we are without the bold voices who once spoke on behalf of a righteous God. We are in need of a mighty showdown between light and darkness!

Many wonder what has happened to our nation. It is simple. We have devalued life, turned Christianity into a political platform, and persecuted those who speak absolute truth. What many do not understand is that our nation didn't change overnight. It changed when holiness became odd and much of the church decided it would be offensive to declare biblical truth. The question we must ask is, "Dare we continue like this?" Dare we think we can survive in a culture that has all but relegated God to our currency, elections, foul language, and religious ceremonies? Can we continue to do life without a deep encounter with a mighty God? These questions will be considered an affront to the religious and condemnation to the satisfied, but we believe that now more than ever the bride and the church must awaken out of its fleshly stupor and once again become the voice of freedom.

Now more than ever it is time for the bride of Christ to do as the prophet Isaiah said and "cry aloud" and "spare not" (Isa. 58:1, KJV)! Where are the voices who will speak up and say, "Enough is enough"? How long will we waver between two opinions? We must change the narrative being presented by those who share memories of yesterday's glory but lack the humility to have a fresh encounter with a Savior whose mercies are "new every morning" (Lam. 3:23)! We must determine that crying out for revival matters more than the retribution of the religiously satisfied and those who represent the church's lost holiness.

THE CONFRONTATION IS COMING!

We need the Elijahs to arise and awaken the church. Elijah was a mighty prophet who stood up to Jezebel, Ahab, and the false prophets of Baal. He also rebuilt the broken-down altars that were covered in dust (1 Kings 18:30). It took a courageous prophet of God to confront his culture and repair the altar!

Elijah boldly challenged the prophets of Baal on Mount Carmel, and it brought forth an awesome response from God. The Bible says Elijah stood alone facing Jezebel's prophets. Her servants of Baal were leading the people away from the true and living God and torturing the anointed, so Elijah declared to the people of Israel, "How long will you waver between two opinions? If the LORD is God, follow him; but if Baal is God, follow him" (1 Kings 18:21).

The people were so stunned by his words Scripture says they said nothing after Elijah's challenge (1 Kings 18:21). This confrontation between the prophet of God and the prophets of Baal would mark the beginning of the end of the wicked leaders Jezebel and Ahab. But something had to take place first so that God would show up.

The Bible says in 1 Kings 18:30, "Then Elijah said to all the people, 'Come here to me.' They came to him, and he repaired the altar of the Lord, which had been torn down." Then came the showdown: God vs. Satan. Righteousness vs. works. Holiness vs. perversion.

Elijah had already set the rules of engagement, saying:

> Get two bulls for us. Let Baal's prophets choose one for themselves, and let them cut it into pieces and put it on the wood but not set fire to it. I will prepare the other bull and put it on the wood but not set fire to it. Then you call on the name of your god, and I will call on the name of the LORD. The god who answers by fire—he is God.
>
> —1 Kings 18:23–24

The prophets of Baal were in a frenzy. The demons inside of them were frantic. The false prophets did everything they could to get their god to answer. They begged Baal to send fire and prove that they were on the right side of history. The whole time Elijah waited patiently for their circus to end. All day long they screeched, cut themselves, and acted as fools. Alas, when their god would not answer, the Bible says Elijah rebuilt the altar with twelve stones and declared, "Your name shall be Israel" (1 Kings 18:31). He then poured a deluge of water all over his sacrifice and boldly called fire down from heaven. "Then the fire of the LORD fell and consumed the burnt sacrifice and the wood and the stones and the dust and licked up the water that was in the trench" (1 Kings 18:38, MEV).

It is once again time for the Elijahs to arise—the ones who will rebuild the altar of the Lord and reduce the modern-day prophets of Baal to a distant memory! This is not simply our opinion. The last book of the Old Testament also declared we must have more Elijahs arise:

> See, I will send you Elijah the prophet before the coming of the great and dreaded day of the LORD. He will turn the hearts of the fathers to their children, and the hearts of the children to their fathers, lest I come and strike the earth with a curse.
> —MALACHI 4:5–6, MEV

This passage declares that unless we have Elijahs to rebuild the altar and confront perversion, families will never be healed. In this fatherless generation we must see Elijahs rise up in our homes.

The confrontation between good and evil at Mount Carmel teaches us that sooner or later we must have a showdown between two kingdoms. What side are you on? Jesus said in Matthew 12:30, "He who is not with Me is against Me, and he who does not gather with Me scatters abroad" (MEV). In other words, Jesus said it is time to choose sides! If you will choose to draw a line that rejects compromise, then there are so many promises that await you on the other side of your obedience. If you are living on the fence between two kingdoms, then we implore you to do exactly what Hebrews 4:16 says: "Let us then come with confidence to the throne of grace, that we may obtain mercy and find grace to help in time of need" (MEV).

To ask Jesus to marry someone who believes love is dictated by the right circumstances rather than by commitment is to have Him marry a bipolar bride! How long will we waver between two opinions? We must go back to the prayer closet for strength from God to stand as His voice of truth. We must declare that we will no longer cheat on God! You're cheating on God if all you want is your own way. When you flirt with the world every chance you get, you end up an enemy of God and His way. And do you suppose God doesn't care? The Bible tells us, "You shall not worship any other god, for the Lord, whose name is Jealous, is a jealous God" (Exod. 34:14, MEV). He is a fiercely jealous lover, and the love He gives is far better than anything else you'll find.

We read in the Book of James: "'God goes against the willful proud; God gives grace to the willing humble.' So let God work his will in you. Yell a loud no to the Devil and watch him scamper. Say a quiet yes to God and he'll be there in no time. Quit dabbling in sin. Purify your inner life. Quit playing the field. Hit bottom, and cry your eyes out. The fun and games are over. Get serious, really serious. Get down on your knees before the Master; it's the only way you'll get on your feet" (James 4:6–10, The Message).

We are living in one of the darkest times in history,

and we know from history that when the world grows the darkest, God's children must become the light. How can we accomplish this? It must start in our personal lives and in our homes and spread to our houses of worship. The altar must once again be the place where we meet the Lord. The most significant parts of our lives must start and end at the altar. It is at the altar that true change takes place. I am reminded of what one of our heroes of the faith, Leonard Ravenhill, once said: "The greatest miracle that God can do today is to take an unholy man out of an unholy world and make him holy, then put him back into that unholy world and keep him holy in it."[3] If you are ready to go deeper, to allow God to take the unholy out of you and make you holy, if you are ready to go all the way to the altar, then read on.

We truly believe that the great confrontation that is coming will take place between the front doors of the church and the altar. A generation will arise and declare, "Open the altar or shut the doors!" People are hurt, hopeless, and in need of an encounter with a loving Savior. We must rebuild the altar and declare not only that the church is open for business but also that we will give the world access to Jesus, because if we don't, we are the problem.

CHAPTER 3

BURNING HEARTS AND BROKEN BREAD

T HEY ASKED EACH other, 'Were not our hearts burning within us while he talked with us on the road and opened the Scriptures to us?'" (Luke 24:32). Has your heart ever yearned from within for something more? We are not speaking of yearning for another possession, a new job, or an exotic vacation to escape the mundane. What we are talking about is much deeper. In fact, the ache is so deep it can't be explained. This is what we call "the inner tugging of your heart." It is as if something is pulling at you from within saying, "There has to be more!"

Maybe—just maybe—the yearning you feel is coming from your Savior. Perhaps the best thing God could do for you right now would be to suddenly interrupt your "now" and call you back to the altar, back to Him. But you can't build an altar until you understand what God wants to see burning there: your heart.

I (Pat) heard the Lord say to me recently while in prayer, "Will My bride answer the invitation to go deeper?" We believe God is looking for those whose hearts will burn again for Him. He is looking for those who are desperate and meek, those who realize that without a deep encounter with God they simply will not have the strength to go forward in God. He is calling you to come away with Him to a place where your heart will burn within you. Are you willing?

COME AWAY WITH ME

There are times in our marriage when we just know we have to get away with each other. It is in these moments, when we slow down, that we realize afresh how much we truly love each other. In these times of refreshing, romance is restored to our relationship and we gain a fresh vision and passion for what lies ahead. In the same way the most incredible experiences we have had with the Lord always seem to happen when we have chosen to "come away" with Him!

To take a sabbatical with God means you will have to stop being seduced by the voice of man, the excitement of the crowds, and the accomplishments of self and allow your heart to respond to the One who is love. The choice to live upon the altar of obedience is yours. Yet with obedience comes sacrifice. You have likely heard it said that the greater the anointing, the greater the sacrifice, which can often mean the greater the isolation as well. Those who desire to know God at a deep level often have to meet Him in secret. When the crowds were pursuing Jesus, He said to the disciples, "Come away with Me." (See Mark 6:31.)

One of our heroes is Pastor Jack Hayford. In an article called "A Time of Altars" he wrote that altars memorialize the place where God meets us. They "represent the occasion and place where we have had a personal encounter with God. We may not always be able to make a physical altar, but there can be one established in our hearts."[1] Hayford then went on to point out altars that appear in many different forms throughout the Bible, noting that altars can be a place of encounter (Gen. 28), forgiveness (Jesus on the cross), worship (when Old Testament priests offered worship on behalf of the people at the altar of incense), covenant (the story of Abraham and Isaac in Genesis), and intercession (when the prophet Joel called the leaders to intercession). "There is a place of 'altaring' and a price of altering," Hayford wrote. "Altars have a price—God intends that something be 'altered' in us when we come to altars. To receive the promise means we make way for the transformation."[2]

In Matthew 11:28–30 Jesus beckons us to come to Him:

> Are you tired? Worn out? Burned out on religion? Come to me. Get away with me and you'll recover your life. I'll show you how to take a real rest. Walk with me and work with me—watch how I do it. Learn the unforced rhythms of grace. I won't lay anything heavy or ill-fitting on you. Keep company with me and you'll learn to live freely and lightly.
>
> —THE MESSAGE

When we "come away" with Jesus, we are saying we desire to see Jesus more than we desire people, platforms, or plaudits. Those who desire to follow a Savior who often withdrew from the crowds (Matt. 14:13; Mark 3:7; Luke 5:16) will most likely have their greatest altar call experience not in the front of a crowd but hidden away in a place others rarely visit. It will be a Psalm 42:7–8 "deep calls to deep" experience, the kind of encounter that changes a person. This kind of transformation requires that we die to ourselves. Is having an altar encounter with the Savior worth the sacrifice to you?

Paul understood the altar as very few ever will. He faced hardships, loneliness, beatings, and storms that always seemed to lead to a deeper humbling and understanding of the plan of God for his life. That's likely why he could write, "Therefore I will boast all the more gladly about my weaknesses, so that Christ's power may rest on me. That is why, for Christ's sake, I delight in weaknesses, in insults, in hardships, in persecutions, in difficulties. For when I am weak, then I am strong" (2 Cor. 12:9–10).

Paul understood that God requires total commitment. It is as Jesus said in Matthew 7:13–14: "Don't look for short-cuts to God. The market is flooded with surefire, easygoing formulas for a successful life that can be practiced in your spare time. Don't fall for that stuff, even though crowds of people do. The way to life—to God!—is vigorous and requires total attention" (The Message).

I believe the bride of Christ is at a critical crossroads. There is an awakening coming to the land, and each one of us must decide if we are to be counted among those who will be ready. This awakening is going to call us to leave the slumber of discouragement, fear, self-loathing, anger, and helplessness to walk in freedom, authority, and fresh revelation from God. The time is now! Whatever has held you back and kept you from walking out your destiny must be put aside. Come to the altar! Jesus is calling you. He stands at the door knocking. Revelation 3:19–20 says,

"Those whom I love I rebuke and discipline. So be earnest and repent. Here I am! I stand at the door and knock. If anyone hears my voice and opens the door, I will come in and eat with that person, and they with me." Will a stranger answer, or will a bride welcome the Bridegroom?

Matthew 25:6 says, "At midnight the cry rang out: 'Here's the bridegroom! Come out to meet him!'" Be up and ready to answer with trimmed lamps, pure hearts, and ready feet! Jesus will marry a bride, not a harlot. The hour has come to rebuild the sacred desk of glory, to return to the pure preaching of Scripture, and cleanse our hearts with the washing of the Word. At the midnight hour you will have to decide whether you choose life or death. The altar is the only place where what you have been can be interrupted by what you can become! The altar is where you find yourself when nothing else works and you can no longer run from the knowledge that you need Jesus. At that midnight hour the cry from within your heart will lead you to the altar of revelation—if you say yes.

The First Post-Resurrection Altar Call

Psalm 34:18 says, "The LORD is close to the brokenhearted and saves those who are crushed in spirit." You may have no idea how many times God has been walking with you but you were so overwhelmed by your issues that you failed to realize He was there. If you learn to pay attention in times of trial, you will sense a stirring in your heart, a trembling when God comes near and changes the atmosphere. The trembling you will feel is not from fear but the presence of the almighty God impeaching your heart to know Him on a deeper level.

I (Karen) had an encounter with God during a time of great brokenness that profoundly changed my life. Our son, Nate, was seven years old at the time and a great joy and a blessing in our life. Yet as much as we rejoiced over Nate, we longed for a second child. I had dreams and visions of holding another baby in my arms. Family and friends had prophesied that we would have another child, but it had not happened, and disappointment after disappointment had taken its toll. As I woke one morning to prepare breakfast for Nate, the enemy's claws of discouragement and despair once again tried to take hold of me. I felt angry, cheated, and forgotten by God, like we had been robbed of God's blessings and promises. I walked around the kitchen murmuring and complaining, talking to myself under my breath. "Why me, God? Why won't You give us another child?"

All of this still was going round and round in my head as I drove Nate to school. The more I let these thoughts take hold, the angrier I became with God. "I am a good mother, a loving mother. Where are You?" I cried. "Don't You care about me?" I was having a major pity party right there in the car. I'm not even sure how I made it home after dropping Nate off. I pulled in the garage, turned off the car, and began to weep. I cried for the loss of a dream, and then I screamed, "I give up! I can't do this anymore, God!"

In the midst of my pity party, when I was brokenhearted and crushed in spirit, I felt God draw close to me. Sitting there in the car, I heard Him speak. It wasn't an audible voice. Yet I heard Him in my spirit as clearly as if He were speaking audibly. There, at the end of myself, God met me. "Karen," He said, "I'm glad you have given up, because now

I can do a work in your life. It is time to wake up. You are not alone."

What came next changed me to the very core of my being. God asked me, "Karen, if you were on a ship in the middle of the ocean and that ship was sinking, what would keep you alive?" I was caught off guard and just sat there for a few minutes trying to figure out what this had to do with my pity party. Slowly the answer came to me. "God," I said, "on this particular day I don't know if I want to survive, but the only thing that would keep me alive on that sinking ship would be if my son, Nate, was on that ship. I would definitely stay alive to ensure he made it to safety."

Then it hit me. God was trying to tell me that this life isn't always just about me. It's about those we are called to. God wasn't out to change my circumstances. He was out to change my heart, to change my thinking—He was out to change me! He was calling me to a greater purpose, a greater vision, and a greater hope. Then, right there in the garage, a picture of a map formed in my mind. It was a map of China. As I sat there staring, I heard God say, "There is your daughter! There is your miracle. She is waiting on you, but you weren't ready until now."

This encounter had a beautiful ending. Pat and I adopted a baby girl from China. Abby is an utter delight and a blessing in our life. While many think that we "rescued" her, Abby actually rescued us. The end of myself was the beginning of God.

It isn't until there is nothing left of our own strength that we suddenly cry out, "God, where are You?" His response is always, "Right here!" Think of the disciples as they walked along the road to Emmaus. Just three and a half years earlier their lives were "normal." They were living the life they knew, and suddenly they met the Savior! Isn't that the way God does it? He waits until you get used to the norm, and then suddenly He awakens you to the reality that there is more.

After walking alongside Jesus for three years, these disciples were a band of brothers. They had seen miracles and been taught by the Master, but when Jesus died on that cross, they felt confused and abandoned. Confusion was declaring war on their spirit and intellect, and they just wanted to get away. As they walked that dusty road overwhelmed with grief and confusion, suddenly a stranger came up beside them. "As they talked and discussed these things with each other, Jesus himself came up and walked along with them; but they were kept from recognizing him" (Luke 24:15–16).

If you're weary and frustrated on this journey of life, hear us carefully right now. The answer to your frustration is hidden in your destination. The very first altar call after Christ's resurrection did not take place in a temple or a cathedral. It started on a lonely road that would lead to a dining room table. Two disciples, one by the name of Cleopas, who some theologians believe was the brother of Joseph, Jesus's earthly father,[3] were walking on a road called Emmaus, which means "warm springs."[4] This area was a vacation spot.

Jesus had been crucified just three days earlier, and His body had disappeared from the tomb. These two disciples were most likely wanted men and enemies of the state at that point. They had just witnessed what happens when you fight the system. No one could be trusted. Their leader

Jesus had been punished on a cross in a horrific manner usually reserved only for the worst criminals. Surely their every move was being watched, not only by Rome but also by the Jewish religious leaders of the day. They were fed up. It was time to go to a vacation spot called Emmaus. Then suddenly Jesus interrupted them.

> He asked them, "What are you discussing together as you walk along?"
>
> They stood still, their faces downcast. One of them, named Cleopas, asked him, "Are you the only one visiting Jerusalem who does not know the things that have happened there in these days?"
>
> "What things?" he asked.
>
> "About Jesus of Nazareth," they replied. "He was a prophet, powerful in word and deed before God and all the people. The chief priests and our rulers handed him over to be sentenced to death, and they crucified him; but we had hoped that he was the one who was going to redeem Israel. And what is more, it is the third day since all this took place."
>
> —LUKE 24:17–21

Without realizing it, they had just given Jesus His own biography. They knew His resume, but they didn't realize He was right there with them. Verse 21 of Luke 24 says that they "had hoped…" That means now they were in doubt. Their hope was deferred and their hearts were sick (Prov. 13:12). John Newton once said, "God often takes a course for accomplishing His purposes directly contrary to what our narrow views would prescribe. He brings a death upon our feelings, wishes and prospects when He is about to give us the desire of our hearts."[5]

Can you see what happens? When you are really close to getting free, you are even closer to giving up! These two disciples were doubting the promises of God. In Luke 24:22–24 Cleopas tells Jesus that when the women found the tomb empty, they saw angels standing there, but they didn't see Jesus. Likely they had forgotten His resurrection promise in John 2:19 when He told them, "Destroy this temple, and I will raise it again in three days." From the looks of things it seems their disappointment was ringing more loudly in their ears than the promise of His resurrection.

They didn't know it, but they had just seen the most important altar in history. The cross is where everything changed. It is where Jesus became the ultimate sacrifice. Hebrews 10:19–22 says, "Therefore, brothers, we have confidence to enter the Most Holy Place by the blood of Jesus, by a new and living way that He has opened for us through the veil, that is to say, His flesh, and since we have a High Priest over the house of God, let us draw near with a true heart in full assurance of faith, having our hearts sprinkled to cleanse them from an evil conscience, and our bodies washed with pure water" (MEV).

Often it is when we most need an encounter with God that we allow our own disappointment and fears to keep us from taking the steps necessary to get to Him. In order to be God's living stones, we must first break away from the side of a mountain called "Pride Rock." We must come "to Him as to a living stone who is rejected by men, but chosen by God and precious" for we also "as living stones, are being built up into a spiritual house as a holy priesthood to offer up spiritual sacrifices that are acceptable to God through Jesus Christ" (1 Pet. 2:4–5, MEV). We are called to be living stones who will build the altar.

Think about this: the first sermon after the cross was preached to two discouraged preachers. Do you ever wonder why Jesus would choose to go first to these two guys? Maybe it was because they were the fastest runners and could spread the word to other disciples who were hiding. Maybe it was because He knew God was sending the disciples out two by two. Or maybe He knew that they just needed an encounter! He didn't have to go to them. He was now glorified. He could have lit up the heavens and preached to the world. Yet He interrupted two discouraged disciples and said to them, "'How foolish you are, and how slow to believe all that the prophets have spoken! Did not the Messiah have to suffer these things and then enter his glory?' And beginning with Moses and all the Prophets, he explained to them what was said in all the Scriptures concerning himself" (Luke 24:25–27).

Jesus likely chose those two guys because He knew He could trust them with His message. C. S. Lewis once said, "For He [God] seems to do nothing of Himself which He can possibly delegate to His creatures."[6]

When Jesus and these two disciples came near Emmaus, "Jesus continued on as if he were going farther. But they urged him strongly, 'Stay with us, for it is nearly evening; the day is almost over.' So he went in to stay with them" (vv. 28–29). Jesus was about to continue on, but the two disciples made a profound and powerful decision. They urged Him to stay. This is the key. Their hearts were burning within, but their intellect had not yet awakened. Nevertheless, they asked Jesus to stay. Likewise, we must ask God to stay.

The loss of the corporate altar call has led Jesus to wander out of the church to find those who will seek Him. We must stop having church without Him! Too often we miss the moments when He invades a service because it doesn't match our perceptions of what church should be like or our plans for the service, so we have church without Him. This surely must be the situation described in Revelation 3:20: "Listen! I stand at the door and knock. If anyone hears My voice and opens the door, I will come in and dine with him, and he with Me" (MEV). The greatest moves of God have always taken place when the people of God learned the power of staying in His presence and laying aside their agendas. In fact, every great revival throughout history has messed up man's schedule.

We are calling on the "altared" to cry out and declare to Jesus, "Please stay with us! Please don't leave!" Imagine what would happen if we cried out for God to stay and visit—if we shut down our agendas and learned to once again linger in His presence. We might just see the third great awakening!

> When he was at the table with them, he took bread, gave thanks, broke it and began to give it to them. Then their eyes were opened and they recognized him, and he disappeared from their sight. They asked each other, "Were not our hearts burning within us while he talked with us on the road and opened the Scriptures to us?"
>
> —LUKE 24:30–32

Let's back up for a second. The disciples bid Jesus to stay, so He goes into the house and sits at the head of table, a seat often reserved in Jewish households for the Messiah. How dare He? Then suddenly He takes the bread and breaks it, and the room explodes into light as He disappears. It was then that the disciples realized who had been among them. The altar had appeared before them. Now they had access to God. But here is the key: it wasn't until the bread was broken that they recognized Jesus. That was the transformational moment. Jesus brought the altar to their home to show us that we can have a deep encounter with Him right in the midst of our daily life, right at our own table. His body has been broken for humanity, and now He invites us to come sit and eat with Him!

What did this very first altar call that took place after the resurrection do for the church? It awakened the sleeping giants! Suddenly the disciples were alive again. One encounter with Jesus changed everything! A fearful, confused group of people met Jesus at the altar and came away with fresh hope and renewed purpose. William Booth, founder of The Salvation Army, once said, "We must wake ourselves up! Or somebody else will take our place, and bear our cross, and thereby rob us of our crown."[7] In a day and age when very little Scripture is shared and most worship songs don't even mention Jesus, Luke 24:32 reminds us that without the preaching of the Word, the believer is being dumbed down. Oh, that God would set our hearts aflame again as He did for those disciples on the road.

But in order to have our hearts set on fire they must first become broken. The great preacher Charles Spurgeon wrote, "Is it not a curious thing that, whenever God means to make a man great, He always breaks him in pieces first?"[8] King David taught us this after he was swallowed up by his own lust one night when he was bored on his balcony. He knew repentance was the key to his restoration. Surely he was broken before God when he penned, "My sacrifice [the sacrifice acceptable] to God is a broken spirit; a broken and a contrite heart [broken down with sorrow for sin and humbly and thoroughly penitent], such, O God, You will not despise" (Ps. 51:17, AMPC).

It is in the breaking that vision is restored. There have been times in our lives when God walked in and changed our entire vision, just as He did with these disciples. We have experienced times with God when He walked in and caused us to fall from our personal pedestals and desire Him. The longing in a man's breast for contentment will never be fulfilled by fleshly solutions; rather, its fulfillment will be found near the heart of a wounded Savior who calls the man His child!

What did the disciples do after this amazing altar service at a dining room table? Did they pat one another on the back and say, "Great church service. Let's go!" Did they head to the foyer for some fresh coffee and doughnuts? No! Did they jump up from their chairs and do their best to beat it to the parking lot so as not to get stuck in traffic? No! The disciples got up from that table and went into action.

> They rose up and returned to Jerusalem at once. And they found the eleven and those who were with them assembled together, saying, "The Lord has risen indeed, and has appeared to Simon!" Then

they reported what had happened on the way, and how He was recognized by them in the breaking of the bread.

—LUKE 24:33–35, MEV

This encounter reminded them of the promises of God and set their hearts ablaze! Just as Paul told us in Romans 12:11 to be "fervent in spirit" (MEV), these two disciples caught a fresh vision to get up and go. When you have a true God encounter, you cannot help but spring into action. When you take time to have an altar encounter, it will change your plans and direction. And you will see Jesus calling you deeper, giving you the opportunity to see Him and thus become like Him. That is when the words of Paul will ring true: "And we all, who with unveiled faces contemplate the Lord's glory, are being transformed into his image with ever-increasing glory, which comes from the Lord, who is the Spirit" (2 Cor. 3:18).

We invite you now to declare over your home, family, church, business, and life these three powerful words: "Jesus, please stay!"

CHAPTER 4

TIE ME TO THE ALTAR

THE DATE WAS October 20, 2015, and Karen and I had just finished having supper with our ministry board, who had come into town for our annual meeting. "Pat, God wants to tie you to the horns of the altar!" said our dear friend Dr. Mark Spitsbergen. As I stood there processing what Mark had just said, I suddenly heard the Lord say, "Son, this is the next step in your walk with Me." I was perplexed. What exactly did this all mean? I went home that evening and began researching the Scriptures for an answer. This is what I found:

> God is the LORD, and He has given us light; bind the sacrifice with cords to the horns of the altar.
> —PSALM 118:27, NKJV

I couldn't help but think of Genesis 22, when Abraham laid Isaac on the altar.

> After these things God tested Abraham and said to him, "Abraham!" And he said, "Here I am." Then He said, "Take your son, your only son Isaac, whom you love, and go to the land of Moriah, and offer

him there as a burnt offering on one of the mountains of which I will tell you."

—GENESIS 22:1–2, MEV

This story has always stirred my heart deeply. I cannot imagine what it must have been like when God told Abraham to prove his love and obedience by laying his son Isaac on the altar and sacrificing him. As a father of two children and a grandfather, I have a hard time with this story. It just doesn't compute in my mind and heart. And it certainly doesn't jibe with "modern" Christianity. Today we think of the altar as a place to share our burdens, get blessed, get restored, get peace, and get renewed, a place to lay down what we despise or what is destroying us. Yet the altar has always been about sacrifice.

God told Abraham to take what he loved and lay it on the altar. *What he loved?* How is it love for a father sacrifice his son? When we dig a little deeper, we see that this passage in Genesis is the first time the Hebrew word *ahava* is used in the Bible. *Ahava* means love.[1] Abraham was demonstrating for humanity what strong affection between a Father and son looks like. You see, God doesn't just ask us to leave what we don't like at the altar. That's so easy it isn't a sacrifice. He desires that we leave what we love at the altar. In fact, the altar has always required a sacrifice that costs us something. In 2 Samuel 24 when King David went to buy land to build an altar for the Lord, the man who owned the land, Araunah, tried to give it to him, but David refused, saying, "I will not sacrifice to the LORD my God burnt offerings that cost me nothing" (v. 24). David understood sacrifice, and so did Abraham.

Can you imagine how Abraham must have felt that morning as he and Isaac walked away from their home, as Abraham's wife Sarah kissed them good-bye? We are not sure how old Isaac was at the time. Some commentaries say he was eight or nine years old; others say he was thirty. Regardless of Isaac's age, if Abraham was like most fathers, he still saw Isaac as his little boy. So one can only imagine what Abraham's thoughts were as he journeyed up the mountain with Isaac. It was a three-day trip, so he had plenty of time to think. Did he reflect on all the special times he had enjoyed with Isaac—the birthdays and rites of passage they had marked together? Perhaps they had wrestled playfully as fathers and sons do. Was he thinking, "God, how can You ask me to kill my promised seed?" Or maybe he was thinking about how Sarah would react when he returned to say that he had sacrificed their son. That journey up Mount Moriah had to be the most painful three days of his life.

Then Isaac asked the hard question of his father. He said, "Here is the fire and the wood, but where is the lamb for the burnt offering?" (Gen. 22:7, MEV). And Abraham replied, "My son, God will provide for Himself the lamb for a burnt offering" (v. 8, MEV). That is faith!

Still they continued the journey until they came to the place God had designated. "Then they came to the place that God had told him. So Abraham built an altar there and arranged the wood; and he bound Isaac his son and laid him on the altar, on the wood" (v. 9, MEV). Can you imagine the moment Abraham said, "Isaac, I need you to climb up here, son, and lie down and be very still"? As his beloved son lay down on the wood, Abraham proceeded to tie him down; then he reached for his knife. But instead of trying to break free, according to Jewish oral tradition Isaac said, "Be sure to tie me up very tight, so that I don't struggle and defile the sacrifice."[2] This is why Isaac would later share in the promises of his father Abraham—because he too was willing to make the ultimate sacrifice to God.

> But the angel of the LORD called to him out of heaven and said, "Abraham, Abraham!"
> And he said, "Here I am."
> Then He said, "Do not lay your hands on the boy or do anything to him, because now I know that you fear God, seeing you have not withheld your only son from Me."
> —GENESIS 22:11–12, MEV

Then Abraham saw a ram caught in the bush and sacrificed the ram to God in place of Isaac.

This altar experience was preparation from God. He was letting the world know that someday His Son, Jesus, would be the sacrificial Lamb. Someday God would tie His own Son to the altar. Abraham and Isaac were the shadow and type of what God the Father and Jesus the Son would become for us. In fact, nearly everything that happened to Isaac happened to Jesus—from the three-day journey to carrying the wood to crying out to his father to being tied to the altar and taking the place of the lamb. But with Jesus, the Father did not stop the sacrifice.[3]

What does this powerful story demonstrate for us? God is telling us through this story that He desires obedience over sacrifice. He wants to know that we are willing to give Him our best. In this case, Abraham's best was Isaac.

After I received that word in October 2015, I meditated and prayed for several months on what God was telling me about sacrifice. I asked the Lord over and over to show me exactly what He desired of me. I already knew that Jesus became our altar (Heb. 13:10), and I knew the challenge from my friend Mark would require me to set some priorities. Then, on March 26, 2016, I arrived in Dallas, Texas, to host one of our I Am Remnant conferences at Heartland Church, the ministry the late evangelist Steve Hill pastored before his death.

Just before the service a friend of mine, Paul Patterson, came in to greet me and said he had a gift for me. When I turned to see what he had brought me, there before me was a beautiful wooden altar. "The Lord told me to build this for you," he said. This was a divine interruption if I'd ever experienced one. God was loving me enough to continue to stir the pot of awakening. I was overwhelmed to say the least. In fact, I would say that night God gave me a new mandate not only to awaken the remnant but also to rebuild the altars across America.

After the service I went to my hotel and said, "OK, Lord! Tie me to the altar!" But it's not that easy. The journey to be "tied to the altar" can take a lifetime. Let me explain.

GOD ALWAYS STARTS WITH A PERSONAL AWAKENING

For years God had been trying to get my attention. It all began with seeing 9:11 on the clock on a daily basis soon after the horrific terrorist attacks on September 11, 2001.

Rarely would a day go by when I did not see this number on my clock at least once. My family also began to experience this phenomenon. In fact, this still continues to this day. At first I thought God was trying to warn me of another impending terrorist attack. Then finally, after I had been seeing this for a couple of years, God gave me a revelation of what it meant.

I was on a plane heading into Atlanta one morning. As I looked down at my watch, I saw it was 9:11 a.m. As the plane approached landing, it suddenly stopped going down and reversed into a steep climb up. It was a dramatic shift. Everyone on the plane was gripped by fear. Some began to curse aloud. I immediately began to pray in the Spirit. "Could this be why I had seen 9:11 over and over?" I wondered. "Had God been trying to warn me?" As the plane leveled off in the air, the pilot announced that he had aborted the landing due to an issue on the runway in Atlanta and that we would make another approach to land. He apologized for the abrupt change in altitude but said it was unavoidable.

With a sigh of relief and a racing heart I leaned back and shut my eyes. Just then the Lord said to me, "Pat, the 9:11 you have seen for so long represents Psalm 91:1. You have been so busy doing My work that you rarely spend time in the secret place with Me!" I immediately reached under the seat to grab the Bible in my briefcase and opened it to Psalm 91:1. "He that dwelleth in the secret place of the most High shall abide under the shadow of the Almighty" (KJV). God had been using the numbers 9-1-1 to awaken me to my own spiritual emergency. I was in need of a personal awakening!

Sooner or later we all need a personal awakening. No one can ever get too busy to spend time in the secret place. One of the major reasons Christian leaders with great power and vision burn out is because they do not slow down and seek the face of God. Often we think that being busy doing the Lord's work is the same as spending time with Him. I wonder how many people have drifted from God while leading others to salvation. If the devil can't make you sin, then he will just make you busy! Here I was traveling the world preaching the gospel, but I couldn't remember the last time I'd had a personal encounter with the God I preached about so boldly.

I know I'm not the only one who struggles with this. It's epidemic in ministry today. We are busy working at saving the world when very often we are in need of being rescued ourselves. We hold a microphone in one hand and a glass of water in the other, and yet we have forgotten how to drink from the Living Well for ourselves. We are dehydrated and don't know it. It is time for those of us in ministry to make up our minds that we will not wear on our sleeve what we have not hidden in our hearts, that we will not preach a message of life if we have yet to experience resurrection. We cannot give away what we do not have.

This revelation began a transformation in me and my family. God began to call us to a whole new level of intimacy with Him, a deeper place than we had ever experienced. We could no longer do life as usual. God was demanding more of our private time with Him. God wanted me to tie myself to the altar. I, who had stood in front of thousands of altars ministering, was now to lay down my life in total surrender. For me there was no turning back. It was either all or nothing at that point. I had to pursue this life of being totally submitted to the Father at a new level. The transformation I longed to see in those I ministered to, in my family, in the body of Christ, and even in the nation had to start with me.

That's how it always works. The transformation we seek always starts with us first laying our lives and our will on the altar. The most powerful place we will ever be is on our knees before a holy God. As Jesus did, we must disappear from the stage—whether that be a platform in ministry, volunteer work at church, or even the pursuit of advancement on our jobs—in order to find God on a deeper and more intimate level. My son, Nate, said to me one day after a time of prayer, "Dad, we are called to be in the shadow of the Almighty! You can't be in the shadow and the spotlight at the same time." How right he was!

THE ALTAR OF TRANSFORMATION

The apostle Paul called us to live a selfless life when he declared in Romans 12:1, "I urge you therefore, brothers, by the mercies of God, that you present your bodies as a living sacrifice, holy, and acceptable to God, which is your reasonable service of worship" (MEV). For me, in order to do this I must die to all of my own desires and be completely submitted to God. Keep in mind that as living sacrifices we can choose to crawl off the altar at any time. Nothing but our will keeps us on the altar. It is all about submission. Jesus modeled submission for us in the Garden of Gethsemane. He understood the price that had to be paid to become our sacrifice and our altar even when the human side of Him was screaming for a pardon from

His Father. That's why the Bible tells us, "He withdrew from them about a stone's throw, and He knelt down and prayed, 'Father, if You are willing, remove this cup from Me. Nevertheless not My will, but Yours, be done'" (Luke 22:41–42, MEV).

The greatest of all altar moments took place at the cross when Jesus surrendered Himself to the Father. It was there Jesus said three things: "Father, forgive them" (Luke 23:34), "I am thirsty" (John 19:28), and "It is finished" (John 19:30). If we are willing to put our lives on the altar and to say those same three things, God will bring forth reformation in our lives. A personal encounter with a supernatural God is the only thing that will transform us. To be transformed by God, we must leave the bottom of the cross where the spectators stood and climb up the tree of forgiveness, using Jesus as our example. But how do we do this? Where do we begin?

We can begin our journey to the altar of transformation by learning to linger in God's presence. When was the last time you lingered in the presence of God? We must become as Joshua was in Exodus 33:11:

> The LORD spoke to Moses face to face, just as a man speaks to his friend. When he returned to the camp, his servant Joshua, the son of Nun, a young man, did not depart from the tent.
>
> —MEV

Notice that Moses left and went back to the camp, but Joshua stayed. He lingered in God's presence. God is inviting you to linger with Him. I urge you, do not miss those moments! God is calling you deeper because He is selfish about spending time with you.

I imagine that when we stand in heaven and look back upon our lives on earth, we will see where God was continually calling us deeper in Him. To reach the throne of heaven where we will see our Savior's face requires a crucifixion of self. We have to crawl to the altar of transformation. God is waiting there for you. He is inviting you to visit the place of encounter, wherever it can be found. Some of the most miraculous salvation stories have not taken place at a church. My father was a drug dealer who found the Lord next to a bathroom toilet when I was just a boy. You can encounter God's transforming power anywhere. Your altar can be a car, your laundry room, the bathroom, an office cubicle, or your bedside.

Your altar is anywhere you genuinely and earnestly seek God above all else. It is where you lay every aspect of your life down before God. When you do, He will invite you into the secret place. The Master is at the door knocking. How will you answer? Which virgin will you be according to Matthew 25?

MOLD ME, O LORD!

From a very young age many of us are told that we can control our own destiny, that the sky is the limit if we only dream big. The very concept of laying down our ambitions and dreams for God runs contrary to rational thinking. Mind you, there is nothing wrong with studying hard in school and having a strong work ethic. These things are good. But as God becomes greater in our lives, we must become less (John 3:30). The truth is, there is a continual battle for our will that will take place until our departure into eternity. It is the war between personal protectionism and trusting that God is in control. This battle can cause us to stop pursuing God just when we are about to truly encounter the free grace Christ offers.

Many of the characters in the Bible had deep flaws or walked through seasons of despair, hurt, and sin, yet we remember them because somewhere along the way they decided that without God they would not survive. They chose to continually stay in a place of brokenness and repentance. They allowed God to mold them. This is the essence of the Christian life. Evangelist Billy Graham once said, "The Christian life is not a constant high. I have my moments of deep discouragement. I have to go to God in prayer with tears in my eyes, and say, 'O God, forgive me,' or 'Help me.'" 4

It is only when we become resolute and honest about our failures that the altar where we die to self becomes a place of freedom. You may have to be like Jacob was in Genesis 32:30; he wrestled with God before finally building an altar to Him: "There he [Jacob] built an altar, and he called the place El Bethel, because it was there that God revealed himself to him when he was fleeing from his brother" (Gen. 35:7). The bottom line is, God will always bring you back to a place of brokenness so that His glory can shine through. The prophet Isaiah wrote, "Yet you, LORD, are our Father. We are the clay, you are the potter; we are all the work of your hand" (Isa. 64:8). If He is the Potter and we are the clay, then we must be placed on the Potter's wheel so God can shape us into His image and put His glory in us. "We have this treasure in jars of clay to show that this all-surpassing power is from God and not from us" (2 Cor. 4:7).

SUPERNATURAL IDENTIFICATION WITH CHRIST

The altar can be a hard place to find. In a day and age when church platforms are larger than the altar area, when those of us called to be stagehands for God—the ones who open the curtain to Him and then get out of the way—declare a call to go deeper in a church service, it often means we are going to sing one more bridge to a popular worship song. Please do not misunderstand. Deep, intimate corporate worship services are wonderful. Worship is the lifeline of a church. After God told Abraham to sacrifice his son, when his servants asked Abraham where he was going with Isaac, he replied, "I go worship." (See Genesis 22:5.)

Hear this: what we call sacrifice God calls worship! We know that worship plows the field for the seed, but some of the greatest moments we can have are when we choose to steal away just to be alone with our Savior. The altar is so much more than just a public encounter at the end of a service. Paul said it best when he wrote:

> What actually took place is this: I tried keeping rules and working my head off to please God, and it didn't work. So I quit being a "law man" so that I could be God's man. Christ's life showed me how, and enabled me to do it. I identified myself completely with him. Indeed, I have been crucified with Christ. My ego is no longer central. It is no longer important that I appear righteous before you or have your good opinion, and I am no longer driven

to impress God. Christ lives in me. The life you see me living is not "mine," but it is lived by faith in the Son of God, who loved me and gave himself for me. I am not going to go back on that.

—GALATIANS 2:20–21, THE MESSAGE

Then Paul went one step further when he said, "I want to know Christ—yes, to know the power of his resurrection and participation in his sufferings, becoming like him in his death" (Phil. 3:10). In other words, if Jesus went through it, who are we to avoid it? We must die to everything.

Reflecting on Galatians 2:20, Oswald Chambers wrote, "These words mean the breaking and collapse of my independence brought about by my own hands, and the surrendering of my life to the supremacy of the Lord Jesus."[5] We must let go of fear, offense, and our own personal inhibitions. We must be willing to trust God like never before. Only then can we build an altar and crawl onto it.

Think about this: there is coming a time when we all will give an account in heaven. It will be the altar call to end all altar calls. The Bible tells us that on that day "God will judge the secrets of men" (Rom. 2:16, MEV). What will Jesus say about you on that day? One of the scariest passages in the Bible is Matthew 7:21–23, where Jesus is talking about those who will enter the kingdom of heaven. He says that many will come to Him on that final day to remind Him of what they did in His name, but because they failed to build an altar, the way in will be closed to them.

Not everyone who says to me, "Lord, Lord," will enter the kingdom of heaven, but only the one who does the will of my Father who is in heaven. Many will say to me on that day, "Lord, Lord, did we not prophesy in your name, and in your name drive out demons and perform many miracles?" Then I will tell them plainly, "I never knew you. Away from me, you evildoers!"

Decide today that the aroma that rises to the heavens, that causes God to draw near, would be that of your own flesh burning on the altar! We must ask ourselves, "Is Jesus enough?" Is He more powerful than our flesh? True Christianity is proven not when things are easy but when the flesh is fighting us, doing everything it can to win.

It was the cross that bought our freedom from sin. If we are separated from Jesus, then we will never find our identity. We must tie ourselves to the altar!

In John 15:5–8 Jesus said:

I am the vine, you are the branches. He who remains in Me, and I in him, bears much fruit. For without Me you can do nothing. If a man does not remain in Me, he is thrown out as a branch and withers. And they gather them and throw them into the fire, and they are burned. If you remain in Me, and My words remain in you, you will ask whatever you desire, and it shall be done for you. My Father is glorified by this, that you bear much fruit; so you will be My disciples.

—MEV

Jesus is our altar, and therefore we must be attached to Him—we must be tied to Him! Apart from Him we can do nothing. The ropes keeping us on the altar are fashioned with His love, "for the love of Christ constrains us" (2 Cor. 5:14, MEV). God's love binds us to Him. This is why Hosea said, "I led them with cords of human kindness, with ties of love" (Hosea 11:4). This is what it truly means to abandon self and crawl back to the One who knit you together in the secret place. The most important altar we will ever build is the one upon which we die to self. An altar without a sacrifice is a piece of wood or stone without purpose. The altar is not an altar unless there is a sacrifice.

Just as Abraham tied Isaac to the altar in Genesis 22:9 and Jesus was nailed to the tree, we must allow God to wrestle us back to the place of brokenness and repentance. We challenge you to declare once and for all, "Tie me to the altar!" For it is there that you will begin to live like never before!

CHAPTER 5

AFTER THE ALTAR COMES THE WHISPER

HAVE YOU EVER been desperate to hear from God? Hundreds, maybe even thousands, of people have told us during the altar calls at the end of services that they couldn't hear the voice of God. We have all been there. Our desire to press in to hear God's whisper is often what pushes us either to go deeper or to throw our hands up and walk away. Once while praying, I asked the Lord why I had not heard His voice in a long time. He spoke to my spirit and said, "Pat, I have gone to another level, and I am waiting for you to get here."

You see, it's not enough that we come to the altar. The journey doesn't stop there; the journey with God actually begins at the altar. After the altar it's time to go to the secret place because it is there we will hear His whisper. Have you ever heard God whisper? When you do, it will change your compass and put wind in your sails! God's whisper is deep calling unto deep (Ps. 42:7). He will show Himself powerful in the gatherings of His people, but make no mistake: it is in the secret place that He reveals Himself to His beloved sons and daughters.

So how do you get to that secret place? How do you find those intimate moments with the Father? How do we hear from a very personal God who desires to speak with us and lead us and longs to minister life to us? Here is a key we have found: the way we position ourselves impacts the volume of God's voice. The surroundings we choose to be in either position us closer to God or farther away. When God calls us deeper in Him, we must put away all distractions and allow our faith level to rise. As Hebrews 11:6 says, "Without faith it is impossible to please God, because anyone who comes to him must believe that he exists and that he rewards those who earnestly seek him."

Many years ago I (Pat) was invited to speak at the Brownsville Revival School of Ministry during their Campus Days event. It was a powerful gathering. Many of today's top ministry leaders were present. I spoke on learning to walk with God in a supernatural way. At one point I said, "Always be aware that God will bump into you when you least expect it." Then I went on to talk about how much God desires to simply fellowship with us as He did with Adam when they walked together in the cool of the evening. Many people were getting touched by the presence of God. At the end of my sermon leaders and students alike came to the altar crying out for more.

I wandered among them, ministering to students, and after a while I found myself alone in a corner caught up in my own pursuit of the Lord. That's when I felt it—an abrupt push from behind, as if someone had shoved me. I turned, a bit annoyed, to see who had done it, but there was no one there. I was alone in the corner of the room. Then the Lord whispered to me, "You said I would bump into you." The God of all creation had come and literally bumped into me, perhaps just to show me He was listening. At the sound of His whisper I began to burn with a holy fire that consumed me for several days.

Friends, there are times when God will whisper and other times when He will shout, and even times when He will literally bump into you. He has His reasons for everything. Perhaps God is quiet because, as our dear friend Glen Berteau once said, "The teacher never talks when he gives a test!" We have gone through many seasons when God's voice was quiet. In those times we have learned to live by faith and not by sight and that it is in the quiet of the night or in the cave of isolation that God whispers His secrets. The amazing accounts from the life of the prophet Elijah tell us that a believer needs more than radical confrontation and God pyrotechnics. We have found that it is in the blandness of our daily walk that we become firebrands of the kingdom.

The God of the worship service can be even bigger in the intimacy of the secret place. We praise God for the churches that believe in creating an atmosphere for a God encounter through dynamic worship, but we hope they also teach the pursuer that seeking God is bigger than a church setting or a song set. We must be careful not to become a Saul generation that loves worship more than the Word simply because it soothes our demons. God expects us to be different and to "worship Him in spirit and truth" (John 4:24, MEV). He is a God whose mercies are new every morning (Lam. 3:22–23)!

Have you ever wondered why you see people radically touched at the altar by Jesus, but after a short amount of time they seem to go backward in their walk with God? Perhaps it is because they never learned to love God past the goosebumps and praise-a-thons. The altar must be strapped to us, not left behind between weekly Sunday morning church excursions. How are we to be crucified daily if the altar is locked behind the pristine doors of a sanctuary, being touched more often by the vacuum cleaner in the hands of the church janitor than by the people of God? Our altar must be a place where the flame never goes out, where the imprint of our life decreases and the fragrance of God increases. We must not get so good at going to the altar that we forget to take it with us. We must be willing to embrace times of isolation.

The Enemy Loves to Attack the Anointed

Oftentimes isolation is a sign that God is being selfish with you. Our quietest seasons can be the most intimate, when God is doing His greatest work in us. Ephesians 2:10 says, "For we are His workmanship, created in Christ Jesus for good works, which God prepared beforehand, so that we should walk in them" (MEV). We were created for His work! Yet we experience times when God is quiet, just as the great men and women in the Bible did. Take Elijah, for instance. God anointed him to bring change to a lethargic and idol-worshipping people. His very name Elijah—'Eliyah in Hebrew—means "my God is Jehovah."[1] Everywhere Elijah went his name announced his purpose, telling people that he was all about God's business. Yet the mandate upon his life brought isolation in the early years.

What is amazing is that on Elijah's most effective day of ministry, he wanted to quit! He rebuilt the altar (1 Kings 18:30); called fire down from heaven (v. 38); saw the fire consume the sacrifice (v. 38) as the people shouted, "The LORD, He is God! The LORD, He is God!" (v. 39); and then the people arose and destroyed the prophets of Baal (v. 40). Yet afterward Elijah wanted to quit the ministry. Why? In the midst of a magnificent display of the power of God— who had been provoked to anger and then brought the righteous a renewed hope—Elijah became afraid for his own life. Why? Because the enemy was attacking him. The enemy loves to attack the anointed.

Jezebel's mind games had him wavering between two opinions. Perhaps it was the emotions of the day or weariness from the hour that caused him to get so discouraged. Maybe he just needed to steal away and find God at that moment, but he didn't. In the very chapter after he humiliated the prophets of Baal, Elijah received a threat from Jezebel that scared him out of his wits and caused him to take off running for his life (1 Kings 19:3). Wait a minute! Hadn't God just sent fire from heaven? Yes! But the enemy knows when to attack and where to attack, and he knew how to get Elijah on the run. Elijah ran all day and finally fell down under a juniper tree while crying out to God that he wanted to end it all. "It is enough!" he cried. "Now, O LORD, take my life, for I am not better than my fathers" (v. 4, MEV). God's anointed man had grown weary in the midst of the battle. It can happen to any of us.

GOD'S ANOINTED ARE GROWING WEARY!

We tell congregations to pray hard for their pastors after a great move of God has come upon their church because oftentimes the best Sunday service can become the pastor's worst Monday morning. The enemy has a way of attacking the anointed after the crowd leaves and the aroma of God dissipates. All leaders face these dark times. We love our anointing but struggle with our humanity. Elijah is proof that none of us are beyond discouragement and depression, even at the height of a miraculous move of God. The apostle Paul addressed this when he said, "And let us not grow weary in doing good, for in due season we shall reap, if we do not give up" (Gal. 6:9, MEV).

Many years ago I (Pat) had the privilege of spending time with Pastor David Wilkerson at his church in New York City. Having realized that it is always a good idea to learn from God's generals when you are with them, I asked David this simple question: "How important is it to pray before I minister?" His reply has stuck with me through the years. "It is more important to pray after you preach than before," he said, "because in the process of preaching you give all of Jesus away and you need to fill back up." I took his simple yet profound advice to heart and have made it my practice for over two decades now. Whenever I arrive back at my hotel room after ministry, I immediately seek the face of God. Even when it is a bit dry at first, I know the stream will eventually begin to flow and the Lord will do a new thing (Isa. 43:19).

In the midst of a dark moment of attack Elijah really just needed to hear from God, and God knew how to set that up. The Bible says an angel brought Elijah food (1 Kings 19:6) and encouraged him to eat it so he would have strength for the journey he was about to undertake. When Elijah was strengthened by the food, "he walked 40 days and 40 nights to Horeb, the mountain of God. He entered a cave there and spent the night" (1 Kings 19:8–9, HCSB). The Scripture goes on to tell us that in the cave the word of the Lord came to him, giving him the strategy he needed to defeat the enemy.

As Elijah was, we too are called to be cave dwellers from time to time. It is in the cave that God often does His greatest work. The best "man cave" a dad can create in his home is not a place where his children go to watch sports or play games. A father's man cave should be the place where he goes to have an encounter with God. As I (Pat) wrote in my book *I Am Remnant*:

> It is in the cave that God can reshape our thinking and remold our hearts. There have been times when I have prayed that God would put me in His cave, because these are the times He speaks the loudest and draws me back to my priorities.
>
> I call it a cave because God used the cave many times to rescue and restore His leaders. He protected His people in caves in 1 Samuel 13:6: "When the [Israelites] saw that their situation was critical and that their army was hard pressed, they hid in caves and thickets, among the rocks, and in pits and cisterns" (NIV). It was in the cave experience that David began the process of building his army (1 Sam. 22:1). This is where Moses was hidden when

God's glory passed by and gave him the revelation to write the first five books of the Bible (Exod. 33:22).[2]

As he huddled in the cave, Elijah heard the Lord tell him to go and stand at the entrance.

> "Go out and stand on the mountain in the presence of the LORD, for the LORD is about to pass by." Then a great and powerful wind tore the mountains apart and shattered the rocks before the LORD, but the LORD was not in the wind. After the wind there was an earthquake, but the LORD was not in the earthquake. After the earthquake came a fire, but the LORD was not in the fire. And after the fire came a gentle whisper. When Elijah heard it, he pulled his cloak over his face and went out and stood at the mouth of the cave. Then a voice said to him, "What are you doing here, Elijah?"
>
> —1 KINGS 19:11–13

On this day, alone in a cave, in the midst of hurricane-force winds and a massive earthquake, Elijah heard the whisper of God giving him his marching orders. This short passage of Scripture should speak to every facet of the church world. We must awaken to the fact that God is in the whisper. In times of trouble He will call us back to the cave, back to His whisper. On this day Elijah would receive his marching orders to anoint new kings and even his successor, Elisha (1 Kings 19:19–21). And God reminded him that things were not as bad as they seemed because there were seven thousand hidden remnant prophets who had not bowed to Baal (1 Kings 19:18; see also Romans 11:4–5).

Just as He did with Elijah, the Lord will always provoke us to need more from Him and more of Him. Our public altar must always lead to our private transformation.

The enemy has a way of stealing our victories and destroying our vision in the midst of our greatest God experiences. If we live in yesterday's victories, we will miss what God has for us today. His mercies are new every morning. You must do battle with the thoughts of yesterday's failures and tomorrow's imagined agonies. God is calling us to establish victory now! In the midst of battle we must learn to hear the voice of God afresh and anew. True spiritual maturity comes when we realize that it is "'not by might nor by power, but by my Spirit,' says the LORD Almighty" (Zech. 4:6). It is in the midst of the battle that "the Spirit searches all things, even the deep things of God" (1 Cor. 2:10). We must learn to walk with God beyond the altar call and into the holy of holies, the place where God teaches us His secrets. The apostle Paul put it this way: "Work out your own salvation with fear and trembling. For God is the One working in you, both to will and to do His good pleasure" (Phil. 2:12–13, MEV).

God will still speak to you no matter what stage of life, ministry, or even prison you may find yourself in. Take, for example, the prophet Jeremiah. He was known as the "weeping prophet." He served as a prophet of God through the reign of five kings of Judah, and he pleaded God's case against Judah when the Babylonians destroyed Jerusalem in 586 BC.[3] Yet his heart for God and the people was often conflicted. He served at a time when the people were taken into bondage for their disobedience, yet God used Jeremiah to not only admonish the people but also to encourage them. Jeremiah became a fierce voice of the Lord against the idolatry of the day. The words God released through him were often like this: "But my people have left me to worship the Big Lie. They've gotten off the track, the old, well-worn trail, and now bushwhack through underbrush in a tangle of roots and vines" (Jer. 18:15, THE MESSAGE).

Jeremiah made intercession on behalf of the people (Jer. 42:2), sharing the intimate details how of wonderful God was to His followers. He told them:

- "If you look for me wholeheartedly, you will find me" (Jer. 29:13, NLT).

- "The LORD has appeared to him from afar, saying: Indeed, I have loved you with an everlasting love; therefore with lovingkindness I have drawn you" (Jer. 31:3, MEV).

- "Thus says the LORD, the Maker of the earth, the LORD who formed it to establish it; the LORD is His name: Call to Me, and I will answer you, and show you great and mighty things which you do not know" (Jer. 33:2–3, MEV).

Jeremiah teaches us that no matter where we are at the moment, and no matter what is going on, God still speaks if only we will take time to listen for Him. He desires to not only tabernacle with us (John 1:14) but also to speak with us. Throughout the Bible we find God taking time to speak with His people, and oftentimes it was right in front of the altar. God is always calling out to each of us to recognize His voice. Jesus gave us this promise in Matthew

10:27: "What I tell you in the dark, speak in the daylight; what is whispered in your ear, proclaim from the roofs." Jesus is calling us to hear the whisper and then release the shout! When we develop an intimate and real relationship with Jesus, we no longer wonder what God is thinking. He speaks to us in the quiet and declares through us in the public square!

SEEK TIMES OF PERSONAL HEART SURGERY

Many times our burdens can become our worst enemy, causing us to forget how big God really is. We read, "Physician, heal yourself," in Luke 4:23 and think we are our only hope. I (Pat) remember well one early morning soaking session with the Lord in January of 2017 when the presence of the Lord overwhelmed me. I had been very busy doing ministry, and I was once again in need of what I call "personal heart surgery." This idea came to me from a verse in Ezekiel: "I will give you a new heart and put a new spirit in you; I will remove from you your heart of stone and give you a heart of flesh" (Ezek. 36:26).

I had arrived the night before in North Carolina to minister at one of our I Am Remnant conferences. We lead these conferences all over the nation, calling young and old alike to make a stand for Jesus through the power of the Holy Spirit. I planned to speak that evening on what it means to rebuild the altar and have an encounter with God. Our nation was still reeling from the presidential election, and it seemed the whole world was about to burn up. As a missionary to America, my heart ached for our country, and I was burdened by the nonstop bickering going on in the streets. Weary of the news, I decided it was best to not watch television but to steal away with the Lord instead.

During one of these times I asked the Lord to speak to me, and suddenly I heard Him say:

> Pat, I am still moving! I am still preparing My people for My glory! I have not abandoned My people. Can they hear My voice? Will they hear Me amongst their busyness and the screams of the culture? Will they listen as I pass by? I am not in the bloated windbags of politicians. I am not in the thunder or clamoring of empty clouds espousing their rhetoric against My Word. I am not in the earth-shaking of nations attacking nations or the fire produced by sorcerers on Hollywood and Vine. No, I am the one true God who answers in their storm. Will My people answer? If they will simply answer, I will invade their lives this very hour and set them ablaze once again. I will seal My love upon their hearts as I have already drawn them with cords of love. I will make their feet strong for the march to My holy mountain. I am close to the broken-hearted. Soon the whisper of, "He is coming!," will turn into shouts of, "Our King is among us!" I am calling My people by name, the name I gave them before society determined their identity. I have known them before the world knew them. I am calling My people to awaken to My glory. If they will meet Me at My altar, I will walk by. The sacrifice of self will demand miracles. Soon My whisper will no longer be faint to those whose ears have been filled with the cotton grown in the fields of the enslaved. My love demands that they respond to My presence. If

they will not answer Me with reverence, then I will allow them to be sacked, destroyed, and taken captive like the children of Israel. Then they will only utter whispers from their dust.

After this the Lord took me to Isaiah 29:4: "And thou shalt be brought down, and shalt speak out of the ground, and thy speech shall be low out of the dust, and thy voice shall be, as of one that hath a familiar spirit, out of the ground, and thy speech shall whisper out of the dust" (KJV). God is calling His people to be in relationship with Him once again! How will we respond? He tells us that if we do not return to a relationship with Him, we will whisper from the dust. Remember, it was dust that covered the altar in 1 Kings 18:21.

PHYSICAL EYESIGHT WILL BLIND SPIRITUAL VISION[4]

We had heavy hearts for several weeks in the early part of 2017 because there seemed to be an all-out assault against those whom God has chosen to do His work. Many of our dear friends in ministry seemed to be under an attack by hell itself. We spent one night at the hospital with dear pastor friends who were praying for a granddaughter whose life was in jeopardy. We witnessed that night what it means when a family decides to do battle with hell! While at the hospital our spiritual daughter and assistant for fourteen years, Jamie, found out she needed to return to Alaska immediately to be with her mother, who was in the last stages of her battle with cancer. When we arrived home that night, Karen said, "I am so angry at the enemy! We must do war!" For days we had felt the breath of the enemy upon our necks, and for days we had been declaring God's Word and truth in the midst of the storm.

Then, on the morning of January 11, 2017, I awoke with a burden in my heart. Immediately the Lord reminded me of Psalm 61:2, "When my heart is overwhelmed: lead me to the rock that is higher than I" (KJV). At that moment I realized afresh that we have the ability and the right to take authority over the lies and attacks of the enemy. In Matthew 10:1 Jesus gave the twelve disciples "authority over unclean spirits, to cast them out, and to heal all kinds of sickness and all kinds of disease" (MEV). With God's promises fresh in my heart I stood in our bedroom and declared, "In the name of Jesus, I command the enemy to leave the anointed alone!"

Understand, dear ones, the enemy is doing everything he can to stop this next great move of God. And beware: if you're not coming against the enemy in this time of battle, you might just be cooperating with him! God isn't calling you to live a quiet life. He's calling you to battle. The intense war facing you right now means a great victory is to be found on the other side! We challenge you right now—today—to build an altar of encounter and take back the authority that Father has given you! Don't wait another moment.

Jesus said, "Look, I give you authority to trample on serpents and scorpions, and over all the power of the enemy. And nothing shall by any means hurt you" (Luke 10:19, MEV). It's time to anoint your house with oil and walk the perimeter of your yard declaring the ground as holy. It's time to turn off your phone and turn on worship music.

It's time to dance before the Lord and declare a holy fast! (See Isaiah 58.) And then take your stand as instructed in Ephesians 6:11: "Put on the full armor of God, so that you may be able to stand against the schemes of the devil" (MEV). Remember, the enemy does not win! Romans 16:20 promises, "The God of peace will soon crush Satan under your feet. The grace of our Lord Jesus be with you."

GET UP AND GO FORTH!

We all have had seasons of doubt and fear. It is when we are at our lowest that we must realize God is still God. He will never leave us or forsake us (Heb. 13:5)! Instead of giving up, learn the power of inquiring of the Lord. Jesus said, "Ask and it will be given to you; seek and you will find; knock and the door will be opened to you" (Matt. 7:7).

King David experienced his seasons of fear and doubt. In 1 Samuel 30 the Bible says the Amalekites had burned down the city of Ziklag, taking hostage the wives and children of David and his men. With their families taken captive, David's own men wanted to kill him. As you can probably imagine, David was distraught. Surely he must have felt God had abandoned him! We all probably have felt that way from time to time. But instead of giving up, David "found strength in the LORD his God. Then David said to Abiathar the priest, the son of Ahimelek, 'Bring me the ephod'" (1 Sam. 30:6–7).

The ephod was a worshipper's gown, and when Abiathar brought it to him, David inquired of the Lord.

"Shall I pursue this raiding party? Will I overtake them?" "Pursue them," he answered. "You will certainly overtake them and succeed in the rescue."

—1 SAMUEL 30:8

David wanted to quit, but he didn't. The Bible tells us that he was a man after God's own heart (Acts 13:22). Like David, we must realize that God calls us to get up and go forth into battle. He intends for us to take back what the enemy stole from us. The Bible says in 1 Samuel 30:17–19 that David and his mighty men chased down the enemy and everything was restored to them. In fact, what they took back became known as "David's plunder"!

God wants us to plunder the camp of the enemy. Pastors, leaders, dads, moms, grandparents, sons, daughters—arise and do war! Declare that God is the Lord and that He has all authority over your home, business, church, and city so that after the battle, like David, you can gaze upon your own plunder. Understand this: the enemy cannot steal your authority. The only way the enemy can get hold of your authority is if you give it to him. How do you give it away? By not holding fast to the promises of God as Hebrews 10:23 instructs us to do, "for He who promised is faithful" (MEV).

One of the most powerful aspects of the story of David at Ziklag is that this was David's final test before he took over the throne as king. After he decided to inquire of the Lord and pursue the enemy for his family, in the very next chapter he became king of Israel due to Saul's death. Like David, we must arise and engage in war with the enemy of our souls. It's time to put on the armor of light and declare, "Enough is enough!" God has anointed you for such a time as this. Call on the name of the Lord, and you will not be shaken, as these scriptures attest:

> I keep my eyes always on the LORD. With him at my right hand, I will not be shaken.
> —PSALM 16:8

> The name of the LORD is a fortified tower; the righteous run to it and are safe.
> —PROVERBS 18:10

Jesus has already won the battle on the cross. The victory is ours if we will just step up and take it.

GOD MUST BREAK US BEFORE HE CAN MAKE US GREAT

My ministry started in an empty prayer room above the snack bar at Southeastern University in Lakeland, Florida, in 1988 when God whispered to me, "Pat, I will use you as a vessel if you will simply allow Me to guide you." Those words would lead to years of public ministry that began in the privacy of a lonely prayer chapel late one night. I had experienced God deeply at the altar, but it was in the prayer room that I would learn His voice. I have spent many nights walking into prayer only to be forced to crawl out under the weight of God's glory. Our goal must be to allow God to crush us like an olive to produce the anointing oil. This very book started with a whisper after a powerful altar call.

We want to end this chapter with some thoughts from a powerful sermon titled "David's Prayer in the Cave" by

Charles H. Spurgeon. In it he speaks about how God must break a man in order to make him great. Using the story from Genesis 32:22–32 of Jacob wrestling with the angel, Spurgeon makes the case that before God called Jacob "Israel," Jacob had to wrestle until his strength was spent. Likewise, in order for David to take his place as king over all Israel he had to first go through the cave of Adullam. He had to become an outlaw and an outcast before God could make him a king. Spurgeon wrote:

> Have none of you ever noticed, in your own lives, that whenever God is going to give you an enlargement and bring you out to a larger sphere of service, or a higher platform of spiritual life, you always get thrown down? That is His usual way of working! He makes you hungry before He feeds you! He strips you before He robes you! He makes nothing of you before He makes something of you! [5]

Spurgeon goes on to examine six "spiritual exercises" God leads us through in the process of our wrestling. First, he tells us, God will teach us how to pray, because without a prayer life we are unable to steward God's blessings.

> If you can be great without prayer, your greatness will be your ruin! If God means to bless you greatly, He will make you pray greatly, as He does David who says in this part of his preparation for coming to his throne, "I cried unto the Lord with my voice: with my voice unto the Lord did I make my supplication." [6]

Next, Spurgeon says that we must learn to trust God so that when life overwhelms us and we no longer know how to cope, we can trust that God knows. When you can operate from this place of deep trust in God, "you have the marks of a man who can lead God's people and be a comforter of others."[7] Third, Spurgeon teaches that believers must learn to "stand alone" in the face of opposition with only God Himself as our helper. He quotes Martin Luther, who said, "I would to God that many a young man here might have the courage to feel, in his particular position, 'I can stand alone, if need be. I am glad to have my master and my fellow workmen with me, but if nobody will go to Heaven with me, I will say farewell to them and go to Heaven alone through the Grace of God's dear Son.'"[8]

Spurgeon's fourth spiritual exercise is for us to learn how to delight in God alone. He says, "The man whom God will bless must be the man who delights in God alone."[9] God must become our portion, our everything, so that if all else is stripped away, we still have everything in Him. We must learn to leave all our idols at the foot of the cross and allow God to be our all-in-all. Fifth, Spurgeon urges us to fully embrace the quality of godly mercy so that we "may be able to sit down and weep with them that weep, or to stand up and rejoice with them that rejoice."[10] We can most effectively lead others when we have first walked the path ourselves.

Last, Spurgeon urges us to be full of praise.

> Give us a rejoicer—"Sing unto the Lord who has triumphed gloriously; praise His great name again and again." Draw the sword and strike home! If you

are of a cheerful spirit, glad in the Lord and joyous after all your trials and afflictions, and if you can rejoice more because you have been brought so low, then God is making something of you and He will yet use you to lead His people to greater works of Grace![11]

So dear brothers and sisters, we ask you, will you hear His voice even in your cave? Will you allow Him give you Himself and let that be enough? Will you allow Him to throw you down so He can raise you up? Will you walk the difficult path with God so He can teach you how to lead others with compassion and love? If you are ready, God will make something of you. He may be whispering to you now. Will you answer?

CHAPTER 6

DISMANTLING THE ALTAR OF OFFENSE

THERE IS A lot of talk in the church today about revival. We are eager for another mighty move of God to sweep in and clean and reenergize the church, and this is a good thing. There are many hindrances to the move of God's Spirit though, and one of them is offense. Have you ever thought about how offense acts as an antidote for revival, counteracting the work of God and canceling its benefits? When you study the great revivals of the past, you see that quite often strife, offense, envy, and discord are what brought them to an end. Dare we even wonder how many churches have been on the precipice of revival only to have it derailed because someone got offended?

Truly, offense is probably the number one emotion that keeps us from seeing revival. God comes in power, but some get offended when His presence and power don't fit their perception of Him. Once offense sets itself up, disunity follows, and the flames of revival die out. The enemy doesn't want us to be with one accord because He knows what happens. Revival happens!

And when the day of Pentecost was fully come, they were all with one accord in one place. And suddenly there came a sound from heaven as of a rushing mighty wind, and it filled all the house where they were sitting. And there appeared unto them cloven tongues like as of fire, and it sat upon each of them. And they were all filled with the Holy Ghost, and began to speak with other tongues, as the Spirit gave them utterance.

—ACTS 2:1–4, KJV

The Bible tells us over and over to pursue unity:

- "Behold, how good and how pleasant it is for brothers to dwell together in unity!" (Ps. 133:1, MEV).

- "For just as we have many parts in one body, and not all parts have the same function, so we, being many, are one body in Christ, and all are parts of one another" (Rom. 12:4–5, MEV).

- "Then all of you can join together with one voice, giving praise and glory to God, the Father of our Lord Jesus Christ" (Rom. 15:6, NLT).

- "Then make my joy complete by being like-minded, having the same love, being one in spirit and of one mind" (Phil. 2:2).

If you want to stop what God is doing, just get offended and stay offended! Some of the worst tragedies on the battlefield are not from the opposition but from friendly fire. Friendly fire, according to the Cambridge Dictionary, is "shooting that is hitting you from your own side, not from the enemy."[1] Disunity is friendly fire, and it has the ability to bring God's plans to a screeching halt. Unity in the body of Christ is critical to experiencing everything God has for us. We must fight the spirit of offense whenever and wherever it rears its head lest it creep in and poison our spirits.

THE POISON OF OFFENSE

It has often been said that being offended is akin to drinking poison and thinking the person who offended you will die. Our cities are full of people who are drinking the poison that flows from the veins of a serpent called "offense." This serpent is causing a generation of believers to miss out on their miracles. There are great Christian leaders who have died holding on to hurt and offense. Their epitaphs declared how God used them, but their caskets contained more than a body.

Maybe you are reading this right now and your heart is stirred as you think about past friendships or relationships that have been cut off by offense. Proverbs 17:9 says, "Overlook an offense and bond a friendship; fasten on to a slight and—good-bye, friend!" (THE MESSAGE). Offense ties you to the person who hurt you. Now is the time to make up your mind to get free! It is time to throw off anything that is hindering your breakthrough. It is time to get the dummy of offense off your back! Your altar and your miracle are dependent upon your ability to get free.

Why do some people experience miracles of healing and transformation at the altar while others do not? Perhaps it is in part because some can't get past the things they don't understand. The great missionary Charles Greenaway said it this way: "Don't go to hell over a mystery."[2] God doesn't want us to keep returning to the past. He has a future and a hope for us. It's time to move forward!

At one point in our lives we struggled through a tough season that had us contemplating quitting ministry. As we cried out to God, He birthed this declaration in our hearts that sums up the power of the altar and the journey each one of us must undertake:

> Your past called this morning. It had nothing new to say! It's time to leave your past behind and step into the freedom that awaits you when you encounter the one true and living God, who desires to give you wings instead of crutches!

Don't wait! Do it now! Reach out and take hold of Paul's words in Philippians 3:13–14: "Forgetting what is behind and straining toward what is ahead, I press on toward the goal to win the prize for which God has called me heavenward in Christ Jesus."

You Can't Carry Your Cross and Your Offense at the Same Time

It is all well and good to leave the past behind as we press into what God has waiting for us, but only if there is no unfinished business from the past lurking around to derail our future. Jesus said, "Therefore, if you bring your gift to the altar and there remember that your brother has something against you, leave your gift there before the altar and go on your way. First be reconciled to your brother, and then come and offer your gift" (Matt. 5:23–24, MEV).

With these words Jesus is telling us that we must come before God with a clean slate if He is to accept our sacrifice. It's not enough just to come with a sacrifice. God wants clean hands and a pure heart from us and for us. Could this be the reason many of us rarely visit the altar? After all, it is much easier to leave your pain and sorrow at the altar than to actually confront what caused it. Sometimes confronting the pain is harder to deal with than the pain itself.

According to Matthew 6 you will never make it to the throne of grace unless first you fall at the altar of forgiving others.

> In prayer there is a connection between what God does and what you do. You can't get forgiveness from God, for instance, without also forgiving others. If you refuse to do your part, you cut yourself off from God's part.
> —MATTHEW 6:14–15, THE MESSAGE

The altar is not only a place of freedom, but it is also the place to offer others the freedom that comes from forgiveness. It's time to stop living in the prison of offense. The word *offense* in the Greek is *skandalizo*, or to scandalize, which means "to put a stumbling block or impediment in the way, upon which another may trip and fall…to cause to fall away."[3] Unforgiveness is the reason so many Christians fall away from the faith or become trapped in yesterday's hurts. "An offended friend is harder to win back than a fortified city. Arguments separate friends like a gate locked with bars" (Prov. 18:19, NLT).

Do you recall the conversation between Peter and Jesus in Matthew 18?

> Then Peter came to Him and said, "Lord, how often shall I forgive my brother who sins against me? Up to seven times?" Jesus said to him, "I do not say to you up to seven times, but up to seventy times seven."
> —MATTHEW 18:21–22, MEV

This takes forgiveness to a whole new level. Not only are we to forgive, but we are also to consider the welfare of the one who offended us! On the cross Jesus forgave those who put Him there, saying, "Father, forgive them, for they do not know what they are doing" (Luke 23:34). If we are to take up our cross daily (Luke 9:23), then we must lay down our offense because it is not possible to carry both.

THE OFFENDED GENERATION

"Pat, my scars are gone!" Those were the words a precious seventeen-year-old girl named Loren spoke after a service not long ago. As she stood there shaking with tears rolling down her face, she began to share her story. During the service that night the Holy Spirit told her to forgive her mother who had walked away from their family a year and half before to start a new life. In her pain this young girl had begun cutting herself. As she forgave her mother during the service that night, her physical scars disappeared. Her brother and her father were eyewitnesses to the miracle.

That night after the service this young girl called her mother to tell her of the miracle of the disappearing scars.

The next day her mom drove eight hours to attend the service that night, and she was radically saved. The last we heard, the family was completely restored. What is amazing is that the girl's miracle started when she forgave her mother. When God healed the scars on this young girl's heart, her physical scars were also healed. We have seen this same kind of miracle happen many, many times, and each time we are always moved to our very core at the goodness and love of God.

This young lady's story is miraculous, but we have met many people who haven't been able to forgive as she did. There are many teenagers who are ready to give up on life. It's as if they're being worn out by the storms of life before they even reach adulthood. Psalm 55:4–8 describes how they might feel:

> My insides are turned inside out; specters of death have me down. I shake with fear, I shudder from head to foot. "Who will give me wings," I ask— "wings like a dove?" Get me out of here on dove wings; I want some peace and quiet. I want a walk in the country, I want a cabin in the woods. I'm desperate for a change from rage and stormy weather.
> —THE MESSAGE

You can soar like an eagle with the breath of God under your wings, or you can use your circumstances as a crutch to hinder the rest of your life. There are too many believers who are crippled by hurts yet brace themselves with crutches instead of surrendering their offense at the altar. We see it all the time.

For years we have ministered to multiple thousands of

teenagers who are part of an offended generation. Many have every right to be hurt because of what they have faced in their short time here on earth. The stories of abandonment, molestation, abuse, and even murder are heartbreaking. The chaos in their lives started behind the front door of their homes, where the very concept of family and security was foreign. It is amazing that so many parents talk about this generation as if they, the parents, had nothing to do with the state our youth are in. This is a generation where a third have grown up without their biological fathers in the home;[4] that percentage nearly doubles among African Americans.[5] So often when we minister at large youth conferences, we feel as if we are ministering in a triage center. Over the years we have watched these wounded children become wounded adults who pass their pain on to the next generation. Every day we see the results of their pain in our streets and neighborhoods.

We are reminded of when five Dallas police officers were shot dead by a lone gunman during a Black Lives Matter rally on July 7, 2016. The nation was horrified. These brave men were killed while protecting the very ones who were rallying against them. When the shots rang out, the brave police ran toward the gunfire as the protesters ran for cover. During the memorial service for the slain police officers, former President George W. Bush made this statement: "Too often we judge other groups by their worst examples while judging ourselves by our best intentions."[6] Those words could be applied to nearly every conflict we will face. As you stand on the corner of destiny and your circumstances, you must decide which path you will take—the one that keeps you walking in offense or the one that requires you to forgive.

CIRCUMSTANCES DON'T DETERMINE DESTINY

The Bible is littered with stories of offense. The illustrations are too many to count—from Cain and Abel to Jacob and Esau to David and Saul down to Paul and Barnabas. There seems to be an illustration in God's Word for every type of offense. Yet the most powerful illustration in the Bible of someone who overcame offense is the story of Joseph. Joseph was a guy who had the world by the tail. He had the best of everything except for one problem: his brothers hated him. The name *Joseph* means "Jehovah has added."[7] God would always add to Joseph where he was lacking, but that didn't mean he would face no pain. He faced much pain, but it was during his time of heartache that God transformed him. You see, Joseph refused to give in to offense, and having an unoffendable spirit is what allowed God to transform him.

How would you respond if you were hated by your own brothers, who referred to you as "that dreamer" before they threw you into a pit? "'Here comes that dreamer!' they said to each other. 'Come now, let's kill him and throw him into one of these cisterns and say that a ferocious animal devoured him. Then we'll see what comes of his dreams'" (Gen. 37:19–20). And it just got worse. After his brothers threw him into a pit, they sold him into slavery. Picture Joseph tied to the back of a camel bouncing through the desert. It would have been easy for someone to give up on the dream at that point, but not Joseph.

The story continues, and we find him living in the house

of Potiphar, the chief executioner. Eventually Joseph was made head over Potiphar's house because of his strength of character. Then a "suddenly" occurred. Potiphar's wife tried to seduce him and Joseph didn't reciprocate. Angry at being rebuffed, she had him thrown in prison (Gen. 39). Yet after all of that, nowhere in Scripture do we find Joseph taking offense. In fact, quite the opposite happens. While in prison Joseph ended up running the place because of a prophetic anointing God had given him.

But Joseph's story didn't end there. There was still another hurdle of forgiveness awaiting him, and he did not disappoint. Pharaoh heard of Joseph's ability to interpret dreams, and, disturbed by a series of dreams he didn't understand, he sent for Joseph to give him an interpretation. Joseph was able to interpret Pharaoh's dreams, and by way of appreciation, Pharaoh put Joseph in charge of Egypt. That's right—Joseph went from prison to prime minister in one day. His willingness to forgive offense did not go unnoticed by God. If you don't take offense, if you don't let offense steal your heart, God will make you ruler over that which was trying to destroy you. But there is still more to Joseph's story.

Eventually famine struck all the land (Gen. 42). Now everyone had to come to Egypt to get food to survive, including Joseph's brothers and his father, who did not realize he was still alive much less ruler of Egypt. Finally Joseph would come face-to-face with the brothers who tried to kill him. For twenty years he had carried the pain of betrayal, but when he saw his brothers, he ducked out of sight and wept. He could have punished them, sent them away without food, or even killed them, but instead he wept. Then he went to them, and this is what he said:

> But God sent me ahead of you to preserve for you a remnant on earth and to save your lives by a great deliverance. So then, it was not you who sent me here, but God. He made me father to Pharaoh, lord of his entire household and ruler of all Egypt. Now hurry back to my father and say to him, "This is what your son Joseph says: God has made me lord of all Egypt. Come down to me; don't delay."
>
> —GENESIS 45:7–9

The Bible says Joseph brought all of his family to live with him. He saved them from the famine. Why is this important? Joseph had a brother named Levi, who had a daughter named Jochebed. Jochebed would become the mother of Moses, the deliverer of Israel.[8] How you handle offense today will determine the heroes of tomorrow. Your future is not dependent on the offense. Your future is dependent on your response to the offense. As it was with Joseph, your surroundings don't have to determine your destiny.

ARE YOU HINDERING YOUR ALTAR EXPERIENCE?

I (Pat) have always loved the altar. I live for encounters with God. Nevertheless, I was in ministry for years before I realized that something was hindering my altar experience. It was offense.

I spent so many years offended I'm not even sure when it began. Maybe it was the church culture I was raised in that helped to foster my offended spirit. My parents became believers when I was very young and almost immediately went into ministry. Those early years as a pastor's kid were tough. We moved to several different churches, and I experienced a great deal of disappointment and heartache at each one. There seemed to be more gossip and division at the next church than at the last, which set up a spirit of offense in me that for many years I didn't even know existed.

My childhood years gave way to adulthood, and life was good. I married an amazing lady and began traveling the world ministering to thousands, yet all the while I was living offended. Some of it was subtle, but an incident that occurred several years ago seemed to bring it to a head. The situation involved people outside my family, but it hit me very personally and seemed to take the wind out of my sails. My family noticed that I just wasn't the same anymore. I had lost my joy for ministry and, it seemed, for life. I had trouble sharing future vision because I lived in the past. I was so grieved, I was constantly battling discouragement. My family began to tiptoe around me because they could tell I was in pain, and they didn't want to aggravate the wound.

I remember the moment I decided enough was enough. The date was October 13, 2013. After arriving home from a speaking engagement, I went to the local high school football field to meet Karen and our daughter, Abby. While Abby was on the field participating in her cheerleading practice, Karen and I planned to watch her and enjoy the lovely fall weather.

This field was a place of special memories. Our son had

played football there throughout junior and senior high school. We had stood in the stands many a night, cheering him on through epic gridiron battles and holding our breath on last-minute field goals, touchdowns, and even injuries. We had built many relationships in those stands as we talked with other parents. I had even preached on that field one night.

On this particular evening it was beautiful outside. As we began our stroll, I looked across the courtyard toward where Abby was practicing. Karen saw the pain on my face and realized my thoughts were somewhere else. Turning to me, she said, "I want the old Pat back. You laugh, you smile, you minister and love everyone around you, but I can tell you are not really you."

Tears filled my eyes. She was right. I wanted to brush off what she was saying and tell her, "No, I am fine," but we have a rule that we never lie to each other. Then suddenly it hit me. My family was living in the same prison I was in. My offense had imprisoned them with me. I had spent my life preaching forgiveness and redemption in all situations, but I myself was being held hostage, and my family was suffering with me.

At that moment, standing in the end zone of the very football field where our family had experienced so many good memories, I took Karen by the hand and said, "OK! Here is what we are going to do. We are going to walk to the other end zone. If God doesn't take my hurt away by the time we get there, then I will quit the ministry."

"OK," Karen replied. "Let's walk. I believe God will restore you."

As we began the 100-yard journey, I started to weep.

Suddenly I began quoting Scripture and praying out aloud in the Spirit. I felt like everyone could hear me, but I didn't care. As we approached the 50-yard line, I said to Karen, with tears running down my face, "We are halfway there." I was having a Philippians 3:13 moment where I was forgetting what was behind me. We continued to walk, and the scriptures and prayers continued to pour out of me, this time louder than before. Then we were at the end zone. As we stepped across the goal line together, I experienced instant deliverance and freedom. It was if the clouds parted. The football field became my altar of encounter. My old man died and a new man suddenly lived. All offense was gone! The glory of the Lord poured out, setting me free. My pain had come to an end!

Since that day I have never walked with a spirit of offense. My children have their dad back, my wife has her husband back, and my Father in heaven has His representative back. Now Karen and I pray this simple prayer each day: "Lord, we choose to forgive in advance of any offense." These words serve to guard our hearts so we can walk in freedom. As ministers of the gospel we must guard our lives from impurity and selfish desires. If we stand wounded and preach out of our pain, we can infect others with our "disease." The gospel is more than worthy of our efforts to stand clean before the Lord every day through His grace.

The anointing we carry will never reach maturity until we offer the same grace to others that God extended to us, and this will allow us to relinquish our past. We are all saved by God's grace. Ephesians 2:8 makes that perfectly clear: "For it is by grace you have been saved, through faith—and this is not from yourselves, it is the gift of God." Grace is a beautiful thing. It means unmerited favor. We can't earn it. Jesus gave it to us when He pardoned our sins. Grace saved you, and to forgive is to release grace!

Jesus reminded us of this in Mark 11:25, where He said, "And whenever you stand praying, forgive, if you have anything against anyone, so that your Father also who is in heaven may forgive you your trespasses" (ESV). The apostle Paul took it one step further when he wrote, "Bear with each other and forgive one another if any of you has a grievance against someone. Forgive as the Lord forgave you. And over all these virtues put on love, which binds them all together in perfect unity" (Col. 3:13–14).

What Paul is saying here is that the grace you offer others should be in direct correlation to the grace you have received. When you forgive others, you're actually giving them the ticket to their own freedom. As you forgive, you empower them to forgive, and the gift just keeps on giving. One of my favorite quotes from C. S. Lewis is, "To be a Christian means to forgive the inexcusable because God has forgiven the inexcusable in you." [9]

Your family deserves the real you, and so do those you are called to minister to. It's time to get free! If you are battling offense, now is the time to relinquish your past and approach the altar. "Humble yourselves under the mighty hand of God, that He may exalt you in due time. Cast all your care upon Him, because He cares for you" (1 Pet. 5:6–7, MEV). You can learn to dance again, just as we have. If you choose to let go of offense and forgive, you can change lament into celebration and declare as the psalmist did, "You ripped off my black mourning band and decked me with wildflowers. I'm about to burst with song; I can't keep quiet about you. GOD, my God, I can't thank you enough" (Ps. 30:12, THE MESSAGE).

CHAPTER 7

WHEN TOMORROW BECOMES TODAY

T HROUGHOUT THE BIBLE we find some of the greatest altar calls taking place outside the physical church building, yet many of us today are stuck in the mind-set that God will only move inside the walls of a church. We plod along in our Christian walk, frustrated and discouraged, thinking that in order to receive our healing, deliverance, or freedom we have to wait for the next church service or the next altar call. We spend week after week hoping our moment will come the next Sunday or in the Monday night prayer meeting or the Wednesday gathering.

We are constantly looking to tomorrow for that mighty encounter with God while squandering today. Appointed times for gathering together with other believers are important. The Bible tells us not to forsake the assembling of ourselves together (Heb. 10:25). However, it is unhealthy for us to approach the altar or press in to God's presence solely at these gatherings. We cannot go from Sunday to Sunday, having only one conversation with God a week. Living like this is akin to eating one meal on Sunday and wondering why you are starving and lacking in health and strength the rest of the week. Too many of us spend our week just surviving, trying to make it until our next Sunday "meal," instead of thriving in Christ. But the good news is that we don't have to wait for Sunday or some other special day to encounter God. We can encounter God anywhere, anyplace, anytime. All it takes is being desperate for His presence.

Abraham encountered God on the top of the mountain when he put his hope and trust in God instead of his own dreams and desires. Instead of building an altar to what he wanted, he built an altar and gave God what He wanted. (See Genesis 12:1–8.) In Joshua 22, when the Reubenites, Gadites, and the half-tribe of Manasseh dishonored the Lord by building an altar facing the land of Canaan, the entire congregation of Israel went to them and said, "What is this unfaithful act which you have committed against the God of Israel, turning away from following the LORD this day, by building yourselves an altar, to rebel against the LORD this day?" (vv. 16–18, NASB). They knew the power of the altar. It wasn't to be a once-a-week experience; it was to be a lifestyle of pursuing what God wants *of* us and not merely what He can do *for* us.

Is it time for your altar to become about what God wants from you instead of what He can do for you? Don't wait until next Sunday or even tomorrow to meet God at the altar. Tomorrow can be the thief of today's miracles. What is keeping you from having your altar experience today? Are you waiting for your circumstances to change? Are you waiting for the right sermon or the right worship song? Is today inconvenient? Do you really think tomorrow will be more convenient? Let today be your tomorrow—choose to meet God at the altar wherever you are right now. The altar is not a pile of wood or stone; it is an encounter with the living God that takes place in our hearts and marks a change in our lives. It is where we surrender ourselves fully to God, allowing old habits and ways of thinking to die so new life can begin. If you are waiting on tomorrow to meet God at the altar, then likely you are missing your moment. God desires to meet you today! He has something for you right now.

Moses encountered God through a burning bush on the back side of a desert when he came to the end of himself (Exod. 3), and he went on to be used by God to rescue His people. Jacob encountered God on a lonely road when he wrestled with his past; as a result, God changed his name and restored his family (Gen. 32:22–32). Isaiah encountered God while running for his life and was forever changed as he declared, "Woe is me!" (See Isaiah 6.) God then used Isaiah as a prophet to the nations. Even though they were outside the "church," as soon as these men decided to abandon their own desires, surrender all to God, and listen to what He was saying, they encountered the true and living God.

Just as He did for these men of the Bible, God has a "today" for you—a moment in time when He reveals Himself to you so radically that it changes the course of your future. So why wait until tomorrow to meet with Him?

Waiting for tomorrow is simply a way of putting off the God encounter that might require us to change. "Tomorrow I will start again," we declare. "Tomorrow I will do better." "Tomorrow will be my opportunity." We are so busy making these declarations that we fail to notice that, once again, today has left us disappointed, weary, and disgruntled. We have allowed tomorrow to steal what God has for us today.

I (Karen) spent the majority of the first half of my life with tomorrow as my nemesis. I wasted years waiting for my turn, my promises, and my opportunities. I was busy waiting for God to use me, waiting for my purpose to emerge, and all the while God was waiting on me to get up and run to Him! I should have heeded the words of the apostle Paul:

> Make sure that you don't get so absorbed and exhausted in taking care of all your day-by-day obligations that you lose track of the time and doze off, oblivious to God. The night is about over, dawn is about to break. Be up and awake to what God is doing! God is putting the finishing touches on the salvation work he began when we first believed. We can't afford to waste a minute, must not squander these precious daylight hours in frivolity and indulgence, in sleeping around and dissipation, in bickering and grabbing everything in sight. Get out of bed and get dressed! Don't loiter and linger, waiting until the very last minute. Dress yourselves in Christ, and be up and about!
> —ROMANS 13:11–14, THE MESSAGE

Friends, it's time to wake up. God is calling you to action. He is waiting for you to get up and move. "Get out of bed and get dressed! Don't loiter and linger, waiting until the very last minute. Dress yourselves in Christ, and be up and about!" It's time to answer God's call to action. It's time for believers to become passionate about meeting God at the altar if we are to see this nation awakened to God's presence once again. If you miss your moment, future generations will be deprived of the opportunity to testify about the freedom you delivered to your family.

Don't wait any longer. Seize what God has for you now. Stop worrying about what others will think of you. Don't worry about stepping on toes. When you seize your moment, you will find yourself so busy stomping on the enemy that there will be no time to worry about the toes of others. Leave those worries to God. He is standing by patiently waiting on you to realize that you are the change the world needs. It's time to say yes to God as you wave good-bye to the lies of hell that tell you to "just wait until tomorrow." God is calling you to walk in freedom, authority, and fresh revelation, but you can't begin that walk until you are desperate to change, to throw aside your tomorrow and your old ways of thinking.

CONFRONT YOUR TOMORROW MIND-SET TODAY

I love the biblical account of Jesus confronting a "tomorrow" mind-set that is found in the fifth chapter of John.

> Soon another Feast came around and Jesus was back in Jerusalem. Near the Sheep Gate in Jerusalem there was a pool, in Hebrew called Bethesda, with five alcoves. One man had been an invalid there for thirty-eight years. When Jesus saw him stretched

out by the pool and knew how long he had been there, he said, "Do you want to get well?"

—John 5:1–6, The Message

"Do you want to get well?" That seems like an odd question to ask a man who had been waiting thirty-eight years to get healed. He had been sitting by the pool waiting for his "tomorrow" for nearly forty years. He was stuck thinking his miracle was coming one day in the future and missing out on what God had for him in the present.

Notice that Scripture says Jesus walked past the sheep gate to get to the pool. The sheep gate was the gate through which the sacrificial lambs entered the street to be paraded to the altar. This man had been sitting very close to the altar of sacrifice for thirty-eight years, and yet he did not experience his altar, the place where he could encounter God's power and presence and be changed.

Then along came Jesus, the very Lamb who would become the ultimate sacrifice for our sins. Jesus walked past the place where the sacrificial lambs were kept and made His way to the pool of Bethesda. The word *Bethesda* means "house of mercy"[1] or house of grace.[2] The pool of Bethesda had five porches or colonnades where the sick were divided into groups of wounded, lame, crippled, and diseased. This sounds a bit like our society today, doesn't it? Our culture wants to isolate us and divide us based on our social and economic standing. We are grouped and labeled, separated by categories such as divorced, failure, fatherless, abused, abandoned, and so on.

The truth is, we are all broken and bruised in some form or fashion, but some of us choose to live as overcomers instead of victims because we understand that Christ died so that we may have life and have it more abundantly (John 10:10). Just like the invalid who lay right next to his healing for thirty-eight years, we too get stuck even though our healing is right in front of us. Jesus wants to know, "Do you want to get well?"

Let's take a moment to look more closely at what was going on at the pool at Bethesda. It was here that the sick, crippled, and diseased would camp out all day every day, waiting for their tomorrow to come. The belief was that periodically an angel would come down and stir the water, and the first one to get into the water would be healed of all disease. It was a first come, first served situation. It is amazing that this place was called the house of mercy and grace when it was completely dependent on works. The people seeking healing had to compete with one another for their altar moment. Is this a picture of the church today? Is the church busy competing with the world, trying to prove its relevance to the culture, instead of being the moral compass of God? If this is true, then we are failing to show the world what true grace and mercy look like.

True grace from God is empowering. If you're not at a place spiritually that is empowering you, then you are not living in God's grace. True grace gives us the ability to say good-bye to the past, to our sin, to failures and pain. As the apostle Paul wrote:

> All that passing laws against sin did was produce more lawbreakers. But sin didn't, and doesn't, have a chance in competition with the aggressive forgiveness we call grace. When it's sin versus grace, grace

wins hands down. All sin can do is threaten us with death, and that's the end of it. Grace, because God is putting everything together again through the Messiah, invites us into life—a life that goes on and on and on, world without end.

—Romans 5:20–21, The Message

You see, grace is not an excuse to sin, because Jesus covered all sins on the cross. Grace is the ability to rise above sin and live a victorious life.

Let's go back to the pool of Bethesda for a moment. Can you imagine the awkwardness these people experienced at the pool on a daily basis? It is likely that they knew one another. They were a fraternity of people waiting for a miracle. Are you part of that fraternity? I have been at different times in my life. Are you waiting for the water to be stirred in order to get your miracle? Are you waiting for just the right quote to be given to stir your heart or the right chord to be struck during worship to set the atmosphere for a move of God to break out? Are you doing the same thing over and over again, hoping for a different result? If this is your daily routine, then perhaps it's time for a change. If you want a different result, then make a different choice. God is not waiting on mood lighting or the right music or a powerful sermon to give you your altar moment. God is waiting for your heart to be ignited with a burning desire to know Him! When you are desperate for Him, He will come.

When Jesus walked up to the pool of Bethesda, the people lying there had no idea who He was. It's the same today. God walks into our church services and often we don't recognize Him. If His presence doesn't fit our order of service, we shut Him out. The people who were waiting around the pool for mercy and grace missed it entirely. Jesus, the spotless Lamb, the source of all mercy and grace, walked past the sheep waiting for slaughter and strode up to the water. The One from whose belly flows rivers of living water stood beside those waiting for healing, and they knew Him not.

They were desperate to be healed, yet they couldn't recognize the healer. Have you ever been there? I (Karen) have. I have been so desperate to be free from discouragement and insecurity at times that my desperation consumed my every decision. I would wait for someone to give me a word of prophecy or a word of knowledge to stir up the gift inside of me, and when it didn't happen, I would wait some more. Here is the deal: 2 Timothy 1:6 says to fan into flame the gift inside of you. Quit waiting on everyone and everything else. Fan the flame! If it means getting down on your knees in the middle of your basement floor and taking hold of the tiny flickering spark inside of your spirit and fanning with everything in your being until you have built an altar, then do it—today!

You cannot blame someone else for the fact that you aren't having encounters with God if you aren't willing to get in the trenches and fight for your altar. When I stopped looking at all my hindrances, difficulties, offenses, obstacles, and what-if's, I was able to see that Jesus had already won the battle over discouragement and insecurity for me. In fact, I realized that it wasn't even my battle. Just as God told the Israelites, He is telling us, "Do not be afraid or discouraged because of this vast army. For the battle is not yours, but God's" (2 Chron. 20:15). Jesus is telling us, "Come to Me, all who are weary and heavy-laden" (Matt. 11:28, NASB)!

The ones lying by the pool of Bethesda, just steps away from their encounter, were so consumed with their issues that they probably thought Jesus was just the pool boy. Listen, Jesus is not your pool boy! Jesus is the One who declares, "Peace, be still!" He is the One who calms the storm! He isn't here to measure your algae but to take your temperature. He wants to know if you are hot or cold today. He isn't here to check your chlorine levels. He's here to clean out the bacteria in your life called sin!

When Jesus walked up to the pool of Bethesda that day, an altar call was about to take place. The man who had waited thirty-eight years for his healing was about to experience the living God. His wait was over. His tomorrow was about to become his today!

There is only one place that will change everything—one place that will restore your joy, one place that will strengthen that which remains, one place that will restore your peace, one place that will heal your body, one place that will renew your mind and transform your heart, one place that will stir you to change your world. That place is the altar.

The altar is the place where what you have been gets interrupted by what you can become! Even the sparrow has found a home near the altar, where she will raise her family (Ps. 84:3). She knows the altar is the safest place to be, a place where she can raise her family in health and safety. We should at least be as diligent as the sparrows.

An altar call happens anytime Jesus shows up. As

we discussed in chapter 1, Hebrews 13:10 says that Jesus became our altar. It follows then that since Christ dwells in us and we in Him, we carry the altar call with us wherever we go. We don't need to look for it tomorrow. It's right there with us, all the time.

Pat and I have altar moments everywhere we go, especially when we are traveling. I recall one evening when Pat's flight was delayed several times. It was late and tensions were high in the boarding area. As the flight finally started to board, the woman behind the counter overheard Pat and another minister sharing what God was doing across the nation. Excited, she shouted through the crowd to ask Pat to pray with her. Exhausted as he was, when the Spirit of God overwhelmed him, Pat moved toward her. At the counter he reached across to take her hand, and when he did the presence of God overtook her. She began to pray aloud and cry. She had an altar call right there in the airport. God met her at her point of sacrifice and obedience, right in the middle of chaos. Pat was able to prophesy to her about her children. Right there at the ticket counter she wept and danced and prayed in the Spirit. It was a glorious moment!

Another time I was on a flight heading off to minister at a conference. I had taken my seat and was awaiting takeoff when suddenly a woman rushed onto the plane just as they were about to shut the door. She looked frazzled and frantic as she plopped down in the seat next to me. Immediately she began going on and on about her chaos and desperation. Then all of a sudden she turned to me and asked, "What is it that gives you joy and peace?"

Folding up the notes I had been going over for the

conference, I began to share Jesus with her and she began to cry. Right there on a crowded, hot, noisy airplane she had an encounter with a loving Savior. Together we built an altar at our seats. You see, we are called to be atmosphere-changers. We are a peculiar people who propagate the glory of God. We carry the altar with us, and when others come in contact with God in us, He will draw them to that place of encounter. The kingdom of God is not about words but the demonstration of God's power (1 Cor. 4:20). Now more than ever we need "mobile upper rooms." We need to carry the fire of God in our hearts and healing oil in our hands. It is time for a wounded, hurting, and lost world to encounter a radical, on-fire bride with no agenda other than to populate heaven and depopulate hell.

The man at the pool of Bethesda had waited thirty-eight years for his encounter. After doing a little research on the number thirty-eight, we found that in Hebrew it was written with the letters *lamed* (which represents authority) and *chet* (which represents the inner chamber, including the heart).[3] Thirty-eight also represents work, slavery, or labor.[4] It includes the idea of one's calling or life's work and purpose, for this is the true authority that each one possesses in his heart. Putting these ideas together, we see that this man who had waited for thirty-eight years for a miracle was enslaved. He had been held hostage to his own pain for thirty-eight long years. In my book *Dehydrated* I shared that I lived many years in a dehydrated state. I was enslaved. And I lived that way for over half my life. Then one day, sitting at the pool of my own self-pity and disappointment, I picked up my mat and took Jesus by the hand and walked to my freedom. When Jesus walked up to the invalid at the pool, He asked him one simple question: "Do you want to be healed?" Fifteen years ago He asked me the same question, and I said, "Yes!" I was done with excuses. I was ready for my altar call.

> The sick man said, "Sir, when the water is stirred, I don't have anybody to put me in the pool. By the time I get there, somebody else is already in."
> —John 5:7, The Message

Can you see that this was an excuse, not an explanation? God doesn't want your excuses. He just wants you. I had lived a life of excuses instead of a life of purpose, but one day I decided to walk past the sheep gate of my life and lay everything on the altar—every blame and every excuse. I laid it all there and left it to be consumed in the fire of God's presence, choosing never to pick it back up again. I stopped being a victim to my pain and started living as a victorious overcomer. You will never get free as long as you're blaming the ones who have gotten in your way! Paul said, "Forgetting what is behind me, I press on toward what is ahead." (See Philippians 3:13–14.)

When I picked up the freedom won for me on the cross and carried it out to the world as a testimony of God's power, I found my purpose and my calling. I was able to see beyond myself and understand that my freedom wasn't only for me. I realized that my freedom was a journey that I must walk out on a daily basis, and as I found strength during my daily encounters with God, I was able to be a light in the darkness and show others there was hope and purpose in their pain as well. The Bible says, "Friends, when life gets really difficult, don't jump to the conclusion that God isn't on the job. Instead, be glad that you are in the very thick of what Christ experienced. This is a spiritual refining process, with glory just around the corner" (1 Pet. 4:12–13, The Message).

For thirty-eight years the man at the pool had been ever so close to healing and freedom, but he had no one to help him get it until Jesus came along. Now, Jesus is counting on you to "come along" for those in need. He wants you to walk right up beside their affliction and ask them if they want to be set free, holding nothing back. It's not until we stop looking in the mirror at ourselves and start looking out the window at humanity that we begin to see our miracle on the horizon. I received my miracle when I woke up and realized that everything wasn't about me but that my freedom was at the feet of Jesus. Only then did I find healing and discover my purpose.

It's time to shake off the chains holding you in bondage. Hebrews 12:1 says, "Therefore, since we are surrounded by such a great cloud of witnesses, let us throw off everything that hinders and the sin that so easily entangles. And let us run with perseverance the race marked out for us." Dare we sit silently licking the wounds of yesterday's failures while the enemy plots out tomorrow's tragedies? No! When we have been healed and set free in the presence of God, we can no longer sit back silently. We must testify of our victory to bring others into the truth and freedom of Jesus. You are never an innocent bystander in the presence of God. His glory demands a response from you. We are all in need of a Savior. The battle between good and evil that rages for our souls demands nothing less than Jesus.

CHOOSE THIS DAY WHOM WILL YOU SERVE

You may recall from chapter 2 the fiery confrontation between good and evil on Mount Carmel found in 1 Kings 18 and God's awesome response. The Bible says Elijah the prophet stood alone facing the enemies of God on Mount Carmel and said, "'How long will you waver between two opinions? If the LORD is God, follow him; but if Baal is God, follow him.' But the people said nothing" (1 Kings 18:21). The Bible goes on to say that Elijah called the people to him and they came, and then he "repaired the altar of the LORD, which had been torn down" (v. 30).

This confrontation between the prophet of God and the prophets of Baal was the beginning of the end of the wicked rulers Jezebel and Ahab. But something had to take place before God would show up. The people had to make a choice! It's no different today. We have to make a choice. The Lord is telling us the same thing He told the people of Israel: "If serving the Lord seems undesirable to you, then choose for yourselves this day whom you will serve" (Josh. 24:15).

When Jesus asked the man beside the pool of Bethesda if he wanted to get well, He was really asking him, "Have you had enough?" Have you had enough of the slavery, enough of the despair, enough of your pain? This man was lying in the house of mercy and grace without experiencing it. There is mercy and grace right in front of you today—not tomorrow, but today. Jesus wasn't just asking the man if he wanted to be healed. He was asking, "What side are you on?" Because "He who is not with Me is against Me, and he who does not gather with Me scatters abroad" (Matt. 12:30, MEV). When your faith invites God into your issue and you choose to surrender and trust Him with your life, He is forced to respond to your obedience. The days of being a silent church are over! God is asking, "Will you choose Me?"

What is keeping you from walking out your destiny right now? Whatever it is, it must be put aside. Jesus is at the door today and He is knocking. He says, "Here I am! I stand at the door and knock. If anyone hears my voice and opens the door, I will come in and eat with that person, and they with me" (Rev. 3:20). Have faith and invite God into your issues. Trust Him with your problems and pain. He will respond to your obedience. He wants to heal you, today. To the man beside the pool Jesus said, "Get up, take your bedroll, start walking" (John 5:8, THE MESSAGE). Immediately he was healed. He then picked up his bedroll and walked off. Jesus activated his faith. Let me tell you, it is time to activate your faith. It is time to stand up and declare by faith, "My God has healed me!"

About a year ago I developed a small spot on my neck that would not heal. I tried topical medications, but it wouldn't go away. Finally I broke down and made an appointment with my dermatologist. When she saw the spot, she didn't like the look of it, so she proceeded to do a biopsy. When the pathology report came back, it showed cancer. I needed surgery to remove the spot and possibly chemotherapy. Naturally my first response was to panic, just a little. But then I realized that this battle was not mine to fight. I drove home, and when I walked into my kitchen, for a brief moment panic tried to take over again. It was then I realized that either I believed that Jesus is the healer or I didn't. I chose to believe, standing on 1 John 4:4, which says He who is in me is greater than he who is in the world.

Right there in the middle of my kitchen I began to praise God for my healing. I declared that He was the healer, and I submitted all of me to His will. I began to thank Him for all He had done from the beginning to the end, telling Him that I fully trusted Him with my life and the cancer. Even if He never did another thing for me, I was determined to praise Him for all He had done. About three days later I received a phone call from the dermatologist telling me that they had removed all the cancer during the biopsy and no further treatment was necessary. Praise God! He had healed me! But the healing I received was so much more than a physical healing from cancer. He had healed my heart to the point that even in the midst of chaos and calamity I could still praise Him!

You may have issues and circumstances that have put you beside your "pool of Bethesda," waiting for your healing. Perhaps it is a dream that has died and needs resurrecting. Maybe you have been a slave to your circumstances for too long. Whatever it is, blaming and making excuses will not bring you freedom. It's time to recognize that dreams easily obtained do nothing to activate faith. God wants you to activate your faith. He wants you to pick up your mat and walk into freedom. It's time to stop waiting for someone else to stir the waters of freedom in your life. Stop waiting for another powerful service or sermon. Stop looking for another inspirational quote, tweet, or meme. You have direct access to the throne room of God. He is waiting for you to look up and see that He wants to heal you.

Today Jesus is asking you, "Do you want to get well?" What will your answer be? Our prayer is that it will be yes. Wherever you are right now, build your altar. Jesus is standing before you with rivers of living water flowing from Him. Get up and step into the water. Freedom awaits you. You don't have to labor or toil to receive it. Just accept your healing and leave your crutches, your excuses, and your pain at His feet. Pray for freedom and acknowledge Jesus right now.

When we read further in the Gospel of John, we find Jesus in the temple encountering the man He had healed.

> Later Jesus found him at the temple and said to him, "See, you are well again. Stop sinning or something worse may happen to you." The man went away and told the Jewish leaders that it was Jesus who had made him well.
>
> —John 5:14–15

The man had received a great blessing, and with it came great responsibility. Our freedom is not just for us. It has a greater purpose. Revelation 12:11 says, "They triumphed over him [the enemy] by the blood of the Lamb and by the word of their testimony." When we share our testimony, others will find faith for their altar encounter. It is to His glory that we are healed and set free. Our testimony is a weapon that defeats the enemy. Leave the old life behind as a testimony of what God has done.

This is your moment! The water has been stirred. Get in the river of God and be healed today. And when you are healed, leave your old life behind as a testimony of what God has done.

CHAPTER 8

REBUILDING THE ALTAR IN YOUR HOME

MOMMY AND DADDY, there's someone in our backyard!" Those are the shocking words our daughter
yelled early one morning as we were getting the kids ready
for school. That morning is one we'll never forget because
it is when we began a journey to rebuild our family altar
one stone at a time.

I (Karen) will share more about that particular morning
later in this chapter, but first let me tell you that Satan
desires to steal, kill, and destroy your family's destiny. We
learned that without a divine interruption, even Christian
parents will find themselves raising up a generation that
does not know how to walk in the freedom, power, and
presence of God. The enemy is busy stealing the hearts of
the next generation and blinding them to truth. It is our
job to take them back. We can regain ground lost to the
enemy by stepping onto the battlefield in God's power and
authority, but in order to do that, we as parents must be
awakened to the battle that is taking place in our own backyard. Ours is a generation of dry bones (Ezek. 37), and the

greatest terrorist among us is named "lethargy." Our families need to be awakened to the power and presence of God, and we do that by teaching them how to build an altar.

The devil's agenda against the home is vicious and bold, yet many times we don't even realize when the enemy is at the front door of our house. The culture, media, and educational systems are working tirelessly to remove Jesus from the lives of this generation, and too often those of us who know God just stand by. There is an agenda that has spread across the land to present perversion as normal. It is as the prophet Isaiah wrote: "They say that what is right is wrong and what is wrong is right; that black is white and white is black; bitter is sweet and sweet is bitter" (Isa. 5:20, TLB). While the culture is busy proclaiming that there are no absolute truths, we must listen to the cries that declare, "Someone is in the backyard!"

In the parable of the weeds Jesus said, "While everyone was sleeping, his enemy came and sowed weeds among the wheat, and went away" (Matt. 13:25). Families all across the globe are sleeping while the enemy is busy sowing seeds of destruction in our youth. Are we falling asleep spiritually because we are worn out from the stress and the busyness of life? Know this—while we are sleeping, the enemy is busy destroying the next generation. It's time for an awakening. "Therefore He says: 'Awake, you who sleep, arise from the dead, and Christ will give you light'" (Eph. 5:14, NKJV).

The Enemy Is at the Door

It's time for Christian parents and adults to wake up and crawl to the altar because the enemy is at the door! It's time to become aware of the devil's schemes (2 Cor. 2:11). We cannot allow this generation to walk into the abyss of lost purpose, power, and protection. If we sleep on and do nothing, then the next generation will say of us that we neither protected the presence of God nor showed them how to experience it. Judges 2:10 says, "After that whole generation had been gathered to their ancestors, another generation grew up who knew neither the Lord nor what he had done for Israel." Let not the same be said of us—that a generation grew up who knew not the power of Pentecost!

Our family has been on an intense journey for many years to press into the fullness of Christ. It all started when we began to see "9:11" constantly. Little did we know that God was calling us back to Psalm 91:1 and reminding us that "he who dwells in the shelter of the Most High shall abide under the shadow of the Almighty" (mev). We take great joy in our family and have always worked to keep our family healthy and our first priority. Our motto has always been, "We can't win the whole world and lose our own family." Sometimes, though, life gets so hectic and crazy that things get out of whack. We are public figures, and it's easy to become great at public prayers but fail at creating an atmosphere at home for God encounters. That is, until you hear your daughter exclaim, "Mommy and Daddy, there is someone in the backyard!" Moments like that definitely put life back into perspective and set off your spiritual radar.

I remember the day clearly. Our son, Nate, was a senior in high school, and our daughter, Abby, was in first grade. On this particular morning, as we were preparing the kids for school, a figure appeared in our backyard. Our backyard is fairly large, and we have a tall privacy fence that completely encloses the yard. As soon as Abby told us she saw a person in the backyard, our son, Nate, looked out and said, "There is a guy in dark pants and a black hoodie in our backyard." I looked as well and saw the figure standing there. Immediately Pat ran out the back door to confront whoever had entered our yard so early in the morning. But the moment that Pat ran out the door, the figure disappeared. It simply vanished.

It would have been impossible for anyone to run from Pat and scale our tall privacy fence without being spotted. Yet there was no one to be found anywhere outside our fence or on our street who fit the description of the person we saw in our backyard. He was simply gone. At that moment we realized that our home was under a spiritual attack and that a demonic figure had been in our backyard. We realized that Satan would do anything to get in our home (and he wants to get in your home as well). Then and there we awoke to the fact that it was past time to make our house a place of prayer. With the words of Jesus from Mark 3:25 resonating in our hearts—"If a house is divided against itself, that house cannot stand"—Pat and I committed that day to build an altar in our home.

But that wasn't the end of the story. Satan was still boldly coming after our children. Shortly after the incident with the man in the backyard, Pat and I were out of town leading a conference when we were awakened early one morning by a call from Nate. "Mom and Dad, I've been up all night, and the enemy is trying to take me out. I can't take it anymore," he cried. That's another moment we'll never forget. It was 6:00 a.m. on the morning of June 15, 2010.

Nate was desperate for our help, and we were out of town

ministering. Our hearts sank as parents. Nate was weeping as he began to explain the destructive path he had been on over the last several months since he'd started to be recruited to play college football. We were devastated. As his parents we wanted to run and embrace him, but we couldn't.

Nate has always been an amazing, fantastic son. While he was growing up, he traveled the world with us as we ministered the gospel. He had become sold out to Christ at a young age. So how did this happen? How did we not see this coming? Had we allowed the busyness of life, ministry, and personal ambitions to blind us to the fact that we were losing our son to the world? As all these thoughts swirled around in our minds, we remembered a recent dream.

Just two weeks earlier Pat and I both had a dream on the same night. In the dream Nate had died in a car accident, and we could not locate his body. It was every parent's worst nightmare. The next morning on our walk together we began to share the dream each of us had, only to realize God had given us both the same dream. God was speaking to us and warning us, saying, "Wake up!" With this realization we immediately went into battle mode in prayer. For the next two weeks we petitioned God to protect our son. When we got the call from Nate that June morning, we finally understood what the dream was all about. The enemy wasn't trying to take Nate out by killing his body. He was going after his soul.

That morning on the phone with Nate all we really wanted to do was get to him and embrace him, but all we could do in that moment was to pray with him and encourage him to hold on. Pat was scheduled to speak before hundreds of teens later that morning, but all he could think was, "We have no right to preach; our son is in trouble. We are failures as parents." The same thoughts were swirling through my mind. As the enemy was busy whispering these lies in our ears, God spoke to us. "It's time to go to war for your family," He said. "Let this day mark you both forever with an urgency to rescue your home first, above all else. I will use your son to change lives!"

When we arrived home after the conference, we didn't scream or yell at Nate. We just wanted to embrace him. The minute Pat walked through the door, he ran and embraced Nate, and they fell to the floor weeping. Over the next three months our family closed ranks. We made up our mind that we didn't need another visitation from God where He was merely a guest in our home. We needed a habitation. We needed God to move in with us and reside in with us as a permanent resident. So we decided to build a room of praise, a place where God's glory could dwell among us. Restoring Nate and our family was all that mattered.

In the weeks that followed, we helped Nate walk back into the freedom of an intimate relationship with God. We wanted him to know that the past does not dictate the future. He needed to know that we still believed in him and that we had not turned our backs on him or given up on him. His mistakes could not change our love for him, nor could they change God's love for him. As the father did in the story of the prodigal son, Pat placed a ring on Nate's finger, signifying the freedom and dignity that is ours through Christ Jesus. As we wrapped Nate up in love, he was able to feel the love of the heavenly Father demonstrated through us. That time of demonstrating the love and honor between father and son became an altar experience in our home.

On that day Nate began his journey to healing, restoration, and freedom. God was able to take what the devil meant for great evil and turn it into a powerful testimony that has changed lives. Nate is now a father himself. And he and our beautiful daughter-in-love, Adrienne, lead a movement of thousands of students and leaders as youth pastors at The House in Modesto in California along with Pastor Glen Berteau. Nate is now using his testimony to snatch a generation away from the lies of the culture. Take that, devil!

OUTRUN THE WORLD

The story of the prodigal son is our absolute favorite and is so special to us. Just like in the story of the prodigal son, we almost lost our son to the world. But that's not why we love this story. This story represents the love of the Father that will meet your children at the altar, and it so beautifully shows how we can rescue and redeem our children with the power of grace and love. So many times when our children make mistakes, it's hard to know how to balance discipline with love, grace, and mercy. The world is usually so quick to write our children off with their mistakes, but it is so important for us to outrun the world. It is time to run as fast as we can to rescue this generation, and it begins by giving them an altar experience.

The prodigal son made so many mistakes as he squandered his inheritance and threw away his future. In that particular day and time this kind of behavior would bring a swift and cruel response from an entire village.

If a Jewish son lost his inheritance while living among Gentiles before the death of his father and then returned home, the community would perform a ceremony called the *kezazah*. In this ceremony the village people would run and confront the returning son, breaking a large pot of burnt beans on the ground in front of him. They would then yell, "You are now cut off from your people! You can only come back as a slave." This signified total rejection by the community. The son could return to the village but would forever live in shame.[1]

In Luke we find the prodigal son coming to his senses.

> When he came to his senses, he said, "How many of my father's hired servants have food to spare, and here I am starving to death! I will set out and go back to my father and say to him: Father, I have sinned against heaven and against you. I am no longer worthy to be called your son; make me like one of your hired servants." So he got up and went to his father.
>
> —Luke 15:17–20

What he didn't realize was that his father had been waiting day and night, watching for his return. It goes on to say in Luke 15:20, "But while he was still a long way off, his father saw him and was filled with compassion for him; he ran to his son, threw his arms around him and kissed him." Can you imagine how surprised the son must have been when he realized that his father wasn't raining anger and retribution on him, but rather grace?

Every day this father stood at the edge of the hill watching for his boy to return. We don't know how long he waited, but he knew he could not give up because if he did, all would be lost for his son. When he finally saw the boy coming, he ran to him, and in doing so he shamed himself by pulling his robe up to run. By law a father was to never run to his son, but in this instance the father was trying to get to his son before the community could get to him so they would not get a chance to humiliate and reject his son. I'm sure the village also was running toward the son as he made his entrance, but instead of inflicting shame, they witnessed a powerful redemption. This father did not want his son to be a slave to the sins of his past. Just as our heavenly Father does with us, this father offered his son forgiveness and mercy, and just as it was with our heavenly Father, this gift of love came at a price.

This father had borne all the shame that should have fallen upon his son, showing the entire community that his son was welcome back home. Even when the son tried to explain his actions, the father interrupted that attempt at manipulation by kissing his son. Then he proceeded to give him new clothes, a ring, and sandals so that his family would not see what he had become.

> But the father said to his servants, "Quick! Bring the best robe and put it on him. Put a ring on his finger and sandals on his feet. Bring the fattened calf and kill it. Let's have a feast and celebrate. For this son of mine was dead and is alive again; he was lost and is found." So they began to celebrate.
> —LUKE 15:22–24

All of these actions served to bring the son to true repentance.

Are you willing to outrun the culture for your family? Are you willing to fight against the labels the world would love to put on them to get them stuck where they are? Are you willing to demonstrate what true restoration looks like? Society would love to mark our children as failures or worthless or dirty and shameful, and once a generation gets marked as such, it's difficult for them to find freedom because they start believing the words that have been spoken over them. They need us to show them by example that they can be forgiven and start fresh. We cannot allow the culture to place an identity on our children that will hold them hostage to their past mistakes. They can start over and be set free. The culture needs to see you standing in the gap for your children. Our families need to see that we care enough to fight for them when everyone else has given up, because this is exactly what Jesus did for us. He took our place and paid the price so that we wouldn't have to bear the punishment for our sins. He redeemed us, restored us, and took away our shame. He didn't reject us or make us slaves to our past. Instead Jesus gave us a brand-new start.

> "Come now, let us settle the matter," says the Lord.
> "Though your sins are like scarlet, they shall be as white as snow; though they are red as crimson, they shall be like wool."
> —Isaiah 1:18

It's time for a clarion call to go out to all fathers and mothers, all grandparents and leaders who are desperate for answers. We are losing the hearts, minds, and souls of this generation to the world's system. Innocence is being ripped from the minds and hearts of our children to appease the perversion of the day. We must declare that our children are off limits to the perverse, secularist, humanist culture that is doing its best to destroy our children. We must restore the broken-down altars to our homes and reclaim a generation that is lost and dying without the knowledge of God. We must allow God to awaken us because our families are under an all-out assault.

This awakening begins when we restore the place of encounter in our homes. It is time to lead our families back to the altar of repentance and restoration. It is time to walk in our God-empowered authority because if we do not prepare this generation for the assault of the enemy, they will spend a lifetime needing to be repaired. It is time to confront hell with a bold and passionate message of truth. We spend a lot of time building our homes and our lives and striving for success and promotion, but until the altar is restored in our homes, it is all in vain. The words of the prophet Haggai ring true today: "How is it that it's the 'right time' for you to live in your fine new homes while the Home, GOD's Temple, is in ruins?" (Hag. 1:3–4, THE MESSAGE).

PROTECTING YOUR HOME BEGINS WITH PROTECTING HIS PRESENCE

The day our son told us of his struggle with the enemy was the day we realized that it was time to protect the presence of God in our home as strongly as we preached about His presence in public. Just like Obed-Edom, whose life was radically interrupted by God when King David asked him to house the ark of the covenant (the altar) in his home, we too must choose to say yes to housing the presence of God. When Obed-Edom obliged the distraught king, this one decision changed his entire family's destiny.

Are you ready to change your family's destiny? Are you ready to make your home a house of prayer, a dwelling place for God's glory? The Bible says, "These I will bring to my holy mountain and give them joy in my house of prayer. Their burnt offerings and sacrifices will be accepted on my altar; for my house will be called a house of prayer for all nations" (Isa. 56:7). God is looking for Obed-Edoms who will be protectors of His presence! Will you be one of them? Are you ready to be holy as He is holy (1 Pet. 1:16)? Will you protect the holy place of God?

King David lost his family because he decided to lie down and rest during a time when kings went off to war. (See 2 Samuel 11.) Instead of fighting the enemy, he found himself bored on a balcony and choosing to entertain sin. David's decision would open a door to sin in his "house" that set off a chain of terrible events, including the rape of his daughter Tamar by his son Amnon and the rebellion of his son Absalom. These sins eventually cost Absalom and Amnon their lives. We must not lie down during a time of war. We must stand and fight for our families. The enemy is lying in wait for us to take off our armor so he can destroy our families.

You may be reading this and thinking that your family is too far gone, that there is no hope, but there is hope. You can change the atmosphere in your home. Start rebuilding the altar in your home so your family can experience freedom and blessing once again. Remain on guard at all times, ready to go to battle to protect the presence of God in your home. If you don't fight for your family, no one will do it for you.

David would learn from his mistakes and later write this prayer for his son Solomon: "And give my son Solomon the wholehearted devotion to keep your commands, statutes and decrees and to do everything to build the palatial structure for which I have provided" (1 Chron. 29:19). At the end of his life David realized that what mattered was staying before the presence of God. When David understood the gravity of his sin with Bathsheba, he ran to the altar of God in repentance. By modeling the importance of repentance and staying before the presence of God, David taught his family how to build an altar.

If you want to change the atmosphere in your home and the direction of your family, be willing to house the presence of God when everyone around you is deciding the cost is too great. Long before he sinned with Bathsheba, King David made this mistake and it was costly. In 2 Samuel 6 King David was bringing the altar (the ark of the covenant) back to Jerusalem. In the Old Testament God's physical presence dwelled upon the ark of the covenant, and because the ark was holy God had specific instructions for how it was to be handled. He wanted His people to understand the importance of respecting His presence.

God's instructions for transporting the ark were specific: it was to be carried on the shoulders of the priests. But instead of doing as God instructed, the people placed it on a cart. As the cart was passing over the threshing floor of Nakon, one of the oxen pulling the cart stumbled and the ark tottered on the cart as if it were about to fall. A man named Uzzah, who was not a priest, reached out and took hold of the ark to prevent it from falling. This irreverent act incurred God's wrath, and God struck Uzzah dead right there beside the ark. When David saw God's great anger, he became fearful.

> David was afraid of the LORD that day and said,
> "How can the ark of the LORD ever come to me?"
> —2 SAMUEL 6:9

In his fear David decided not to take the ark of the Lord to be with him in the City of David. Instead, he took it to the house of Obed-Edom the Gittite. The ark of the Lord remained in the house of Obed-Edom for three months, and during that time the Lord blessed Obed-Edom and his entire household.

Can we camp out at 2 Samuel 6:10–11 for just a moment? David did not want to carry the ark any farther because the cost was too great, so he took it to the house of Obed-Edom instead. Unlike King David, Obed-Edom did not consider the presence of the Lord to be a great burden. He took the ark into his home and even built a house for the presence of God. The Bible says, "The ark of God remained with the family of Obed-Edom in his house for three months, and the LORD blessed his household and everything he had" (1 Chron. 13:14). Protecting the presence of God became personal to Obed-Edom, and God blessed him. When you make room for God, you too will be blessed, and so will your household.

Now, when David heard how God was blessing the house of Obed-Edom, he decided to get the ark and bring it back to the City of David.

> Now King David was told, "The LORD has blessed
> the household of Obed-Edom and everything he
> has, because of the ark of God." So David went to
> bring up the ark of God from the house of Obed-
> Edom to the City of David with rejoicing.
>
> —2 SAMUEL 6:12

Obed-Edom had experienced the presence of God in his home, and he didn't want to lose it. So once the ark was installed in its place in the temple, Obed-Edom became a worshipper in the temple. In fact, his entire family became worshippers.

> He appointed some of the Levites to minister before
> the ark of the LORD, to extol, thank, and praise the
> LORD, the God of Israel: Asaph was the chief, and
> next to him in rank were Zechariah, then Jaaziel,
> Shemiramoth, Jehiel, Mattithiah, Eliab, Benaiah,
> Obed-Edom and Jeiel. They were to play the lyres and
> harps, Asaph was to sound the cymbals, and Benaiah
> and Jahaziel the priests were to blow the trumpets
> regularly before the ark of the covenant of God.
>
> —1 CHRONICLES 16:4–6

Oh, that our kids would accuse us of being worshippers of God!

The Bible tells us that Obed-Edom and Jehiah were also doorkeepers for the ark (1 Chron. 15:23–24). There is a call going out today to guard the door of your home, to keep the enemy out! The family of Obed-Edom became worshippers, and next thing you know they became gatekeepers. In fact, his family becomes the keepers of the house of God! Next thing you know, David tells Obed-Edom's sons to guard the storehouse. (See 1 Chronicles 26:1–19.) When you open the door to God and build an altar in your home, not only will your home be blessed, but also you will see generational blessings flow through your family from the storehouses of heaven.

If you want to see God bless your family, then open the door to the presence of God and protect His presence. Lead your family by example and God will bless you. Once you let God into your house and become a worshipper, you will learn what it means to be a doorkeeper, a guardian at the gate. God will show you how to lead your family with integrity and a heart that desires to stay before His presence. It was Obed-Edom's faith, attitude, and actions that caused him to leave a legacy of faith and relationship with the true and living God.

Lead Your Family in Word and Deed

We have personally experienced this reality in our family as recently as this past summer. We always dedicate our summers to seeing young people across the world have real encounters with our loving Savior. Our daughter, Abby, gave her life to Christ at a very young age and has loved God since we can remember. This past summer Pat and I had a deep desire for her to have an encounter with God that would draw her into a more personal and intimate relationship with Him that would strengthen her as she entered eighth grade. We spent all summer leading young people to that altar experience, and we were secretly praying that Abby would have her own altar encounter. We know eighth grade is a year that oftentimes exposes students to new worldly concepts. We wanted Abby to be able to withstand the lies and schemes of the enemy that would soon be trying to rob her of her innocence.

All summer we prayed that she would have an encounter with God. We made sure to worship at home, brag on God, and teach her how to pray and seek God at home, not just in church services. In essence, we helped our daughter build herself an altar that summer. As we traveled together as a family, we saw hundreds of young people empowered and radically transformed. Abby was right in the middle of all this and had an amazing time seeing people healed and set free by the power of God. Yet even though she loved God with all her heart, she had not been awakened to all He had to offer her.

On the first day of eighth grade we decided to write a book of absolutes, prayers, and letters to Abby to give her encouragement and strength throughout the school year. The idea was that each day we would write a new devotion/letter for her and pray with her. When I picked her up after her first day in the eighth grade, it was obvious she had had a rough day. Back at the house that afternoon we had our usual tea party, a time designed to give Abby a chance to discuss the events of the day. That particular day she shared that she knew this year was going to be different. It was clear that things had changed, and she was quiet for the rest of the evening as she processed the changes.

At bedtime we went into her room to say our nightly prayers and found her sitting on the side of the bed. Looking up at us, she blurted out, "I need Him!" Caught off guard we asked, "What do you mean, sweetheart?"

"I need Jesus," she said.

Pat looked at her and responded, "Of course, sweetheart.

You accepted Jesus in your heart as a little girl." Looking right at him she shot back, "But that was when I was a child. Now I'm older and I want to know Him for real. I want to live for Jesus and make a difference and be a light in my school." With that she crawled over to her daddy and laid her head in his lap. Pat held her as he led her in a prayer committing her life to Jesus. It was truly a beautiful thing to see our daughter experience her own altar moment. Because we decided to lead our family not only in word but also in action, our children are able to find the altar and stay before it, and it all started when we changed the atmosphere of our home.

When you decide to bring the altar into your home and protect the presence of God, it sets your family up for blessings that will flow from generation to generation. I am reminded of the widow in 2 Kings 4:1–7. The Bible says the woman's husband, a friend of the prophets, had died. Many do not realize that her husband was most likely Obadiah, the prophet who had hidden the prophets in the cave from Jezebel when she was trying to kill them.[2]

While Elijah was rebuilding the altar, Obadiah was protecting the anointing. This powerful act did not go unnoticed by God. Now the creditors (*nashah* in the Hebrew, which can also be translated "extortioners"[3]) were knocking on this widow's door wanting payment for past debts because Obadiah had died broke. Since she couldn't pay, the extortioners were going to take away her sons (2 Kings 4:1). These sons were her future. Without them she had no hope.

Knowing she must do something, the widow woman ran to the prophet Elisha for help.

> Elisha said to her, "What shall I do for you? Tell
> me, what do you have in the house?" And she said,
> "Your maidservant has nothing in the house except a
> jar of oil." [The word translated *oil* is *shemen*, which
> means to make fat or fertile.[4]]
>
> —2 KINGS 4:2, NASB

The oil referenced in this passage may have been the very horn of oil Obadiah used to anoint the prophets he had protected.[5] We don't know for sure. What we do know is that Elisha told the widow to borrow empty vessels from all of her neighbors and then return to her house, shut the door, and pour the oil into the vessels. The Scripture says the oil continued to run until they ran out of jars (2 Kings 4:6)! She then went and sold the oil and paid her debts.

It would be so easy to dismiss this as just a miraculous account of a widow's survival, but that's not the whole story. The power of this testimony comes when we realize that this woman's husband was a man who protected the anointing! He had used all their money to feed the prophets. She was widowed with nothing to her name except his anointing oil. So when the enemy came knocking on her door to steal the next generation from her, her husband's anointing oil was available to pay her debts. It was the anointing that turned back the creditors! If we are to protect the next generation, we must keep the anointing oil in our homes so that, like the widow, when the enemy comes knocking, we have the anointing to fend off his attack.

Make no mistake: the creditor (extortioner) wants the next generation! He is at the door of our nation. Shall we hide in fear or stand together in a Holy Spirit–revolution? I think it is imperative that we not sit idly by as the enemy pushes on full steam ahead. Our nation is in great need of an awakening! There have been mighty moves of God over the last four hundred years on the soil of this great nation. It is time to raise a standard once again! Do you want to be found telling your children that you stood by while our nation was destroyed because you didn't want to pay the price being demanded? The anointing still breaks the yoke of bondage (Isa. 10:27), and it is available to us. Our task is to get the empty vessels and fill them with the anointing of God. It is time to tell the enemy he can't have our homes, our children, our marriages, our schools, our churches, or our nation. Not on our watch!

It's Time to Shut the Door and Fill the Pots With Oil!

I want to challenge you to keep the anointing of God in your home because one day it will be what rebukes the devourer. Lay hands on your family and declare Psalm 23:5: "You prepare a table before me in the presence of my enemies. You anoint my head with oil; my cup overflows." Declare that, just like Obed-Edom's, your home will be blessed as you host God's presence. As it was for Obed-Edom and his family, let your household become worshippers and gatekeepers who guard against the humanistic culture that surrounds us.

I want to ask you today, if the walls of your home could speak, what would they say about you and your family? Would they divulge deep, dark secret sin and chaos, or would they sing praises to God and cry out, "Holy, holy,

holy"? What would happen if God interrupted your family dinner one night by writing the words from Daniel 5:27 with large letters on your wall: "You have been weighed on the scales and found wanting"? The time for an awakening in your household is now! It's time to go higher and deeper, refusing to settle for less than all of God's presence. If your home is in need of revival, it's time to adjust the spiritual thermostat to allow the fire of God to burn brightly within your walls once again.

I want to close out this chapter with some points for you to ponder in prayer as you prepare to rebuild the altar in your home.

- Understand that your family is called to be different. Do not believe the lie that you must conform to the culture's idea of what a family should be like. Romans 12:2 tells us we are not to be conformed to the pattern of this world, but to be transformed.

- Choose to worship as a family. Learn how to worship through the storms in order to see the light on the other side, because if you can't worship in the valley, you will never dance on the mountain. Remember, Jesus still calms the storm. (See Matthew 8:23–27.)

- Always persevere and push through. Don't let your family be part of the lazy generation that is not willing to persevere to see victory. Joshua 1:9 tells us, "Be strong and courageous. Do not be afraid; do not be discouraged, for the LORD your God will be with you wherever you go."

- Learn to stick together and fight together! Never allow anyone in your family to be left behind. When one is down, rally together to rescue and restore that person. Fight together and win together. "Two are better than one, because they have a good reward for their labor. For if they fall, one will lift up his companion. But woe to him who is alone when he falls, for he has no one to help him up" (Eccles. 4:9–10, NKJV).

- Continually model repentance and restoration. Be the first to repent and lead your family in repentance. Romans 10:9 says, "If you declare with your mouth, 'Jesus is Lord,' and believe in your heart that God raised him from the dead, you will be saved." And we read in 1 John 1:9, "If we confess our sins, He is faithful and just to forgive us our sins and cleanse us from all unrighteousness" (MEV). Your walk with God is a continual journey of growing and maturing in your faith.

- Have daily devotions with your family. Let your family see that you pray for guidance and instruction and that you seek to continually grow in your knowledge of God's Word. Family devotions don't have to be complicated. Find a simple scripture to help guide your family members throughout the day, such as Matthew 4:4: "Man shall not live on bread alone, but on every word that comes from the mouth of God." By doing this, you are teaching your family that God's

Word is a lamp unto their feet and a light unto their path (Ps. 119:105).

- Pray for their hearts to be consumed by God as you model a heart of worship and praise. Teach them to have a thankful heart and to praise God for who He is and not what He can do for them. Our walk with Christ is about relationship, not works.

- Pray to know God. Teach your family that as they press in to know God, He will reside with them and they can talk to Him at any time throughout their day. James 4:8 says, "Come near to God and he will come near to you."

- Pray to resist the traps of the enemy. Ask God to forgive you of your sins as you forgive those who have sinned against you and to lead you not into temptation. (See Luke 11:4.) By doing this, you're teaching your family by example how to listen for the still, small voice of God, who will show them the way out of temptation. The Bible says, "No temptation has overtaken you except what is common to mankind. And God is faithful; he will not let you be tempted beyond what you can bear. But when you are tempted, he will also provide a way out so that you can endure it" (1 Cor. 10:13).

- Pray for peace and joy. Model peace by believing what God says. The Bible says, "You will keep him in perfect peace, whose mind is stayed on You, because he trusts in You" (Isa. 26:3, MEV).

- Pray for purpose. Continually pursue God's plan for your life. Jeremiah 29:11 says God has plans for you. Let your family see you walking out your destiny with power and passion.

- Pray to leave a godly legacy. In word and deed pass to the next generation an undying love for God and awe for His presence. And declare Psalm 112:2: "Their children will be mighty in the land; the generation of the upright will be blessed."

Start building your altar today, one step at a time, one prayer at a time, one act of worship at a time. Determine to be the example that starts a revolution in your home. Be willing to sacrifice whatever it takes to fan the sparks of revival fire into flames. Protect the anointing on your family so God's blessings can flow to the generations to come. Be about the task of building your family's altar one stone at a time. Start by making God the center of your life. Make your home a place that houses and protects God's presence. If you will live without compromise and teach the next generation that they too can have a real and intimate relationship with our loving Father, you can transform your family's future and leave a legacy of blessing that impacts generations to come.

CHAPTER 9

ARE YOU OUT OF BREATH?

"HEN THE LORD God formed a man from the dust of the ground and breathed into his nostrils the breath of life, and the man became a living being" (Gen. 2:7). It is the breath of our Father God that imbued life into us, and it is His breath that continues to sustain us. Without this precious breath, humankind would not exist. The breath of God is life itself.

Throughout the Bible, when the breath of God is present, it produces or revives life. If God is our very life breath, then we should be living in a place of revival, but many of us are not. In fact, some of us are out of breath. Life has a way of taking our breath away. The phrase "take my breath away" typically makes us think of moments when the beauty and grandeur of God leave us breathless, but that is not the kind of breathlessness we're referring to. There is another kind of breathlessness that comes upon us when life is pressing in so hard that we feel crushed and desperate, as if we can hardly breathe.

Maybe you wake up so weary and exhausted you think

you can't possibly make it through the day. Perhaps you feel hopeless and lost. You're certainly not alone. But our God is a God of hope. If you let Him, He will breathe into you and fill your spiritual lungs with His very life and revive your soul. Then, when you are full of God, His presence will overflow to everyone you come in contact with.

If you have reached for your spiritual inhaler on more than one occasion, then perhaps it is time to build a "breathing room" for God. Maybe it's time to create a place for God to meet you and breathe new life into you as you encounter Him on a personal level. But know this—when you inhale God's breath, you will exhale revival fire!

So what is revival fire? The word *revival* has become a buzzword the church uses to describe a great spiritual experience. We are continually talking about and praying for revival. But if we are going to pray about revival, shouldn't we know what it actually is? *Revival* is "an improvement in the condition or strength of something; an instance of something becoming popular, active, or important again; a reawakening of religious fervor."[1] Wow! That definition should not only excite us but also awaken us to the fact that most of us are not living in a state of revival.

Yes, we go to meetings where we are moved by the music and touched by the sermon, but are we in fact improved, strengthened, or reawakened in our spirits? If we truly experienced revival, shouldn't entire cities, states, and nations be changed as people encounter the living God? It seems the body of Christ would be influencing culture rather than culture influencing the church if we were in revival, but that is not always happening. We have become satisfied to merely coexist with the culture around us.

It's time for us to experience personal revival so corporate revival can begin to influence our society. It's time for us to be resuscitated out of our state of lethargy and compromise so we can improve the condition of our world, strengthen the next generation, and reawaken our spiritual fervor so our lives display God's resurrection power. That's what revival is!

It's time for us to groan again that God would send His Spirit across our land. Charles Spurgeon said, "Groanings which cannot be uttered are often prayers which cannot be refused."[2] We need to get back to a place of deep travail, where our soul groans for the breath of God to blow afresh into our lives. We call this the "sigh of the soul." A sigh is when you audibly exhale in disgust or relief. If you are tired of where you are in your walk with God, disgusted by continual shifting winds of cultural compromise, exhausted from fighting the enemy on every front and just merely surviving, then it is time to build a breathing room in your life, a place where you can breathe in the breath of God.

> And it came to pass in process of time, that the king of Egypt died: and the children of Israel sighed ["groaned" in the NIV] by reason of the bondage, and they cried, and their cry came up unto God by reason of the bondage. And God heard their groaning, and God remembered his covenant with Abraham, with Isaac, and with Jacob. And God looked upon the children of Israel and God had respect unto them.
>
> —EXODUS 2:23–25, KJV

Our nation is in crisis, and it is time for us as believers to rise up and groan again. It is not until we get to the point of sighing and exhaling all the things that have so entrapped us that we will be able to take a deep breath of God's Spirit once again. Many of you are walking through battles and struggles, but we want to encourage you because we believe we are at the point of breakthrough! The children of Israel were in bondage for four hundred years before they came to their appointed time. And it is interesting that the appointed time for their deliverance coincided with the season of their sigh.

Up to that point the children of Israel had been pretty content with their bondage, not unlike the United States right now. It's easy to rationalize that things aren't that bad, to compromise just a little when it comes to perversion and spiritual bondage. But then the children of Israel woke up and realized enough is enough, and suddenly *they all sighed*! Suddenly they were no longer willing to settle for less, and when that happened, everything changed. Are you tired of living in bondage day after day? Are you ready to exhale those things that have you trapped? If so, know that your travail will get God's attention.

> In the same way, the Spirit helps us in our weakness. We do not know what we ought to pray for, but the Spirit himself intercedes for us through wordless groans.
>
> —Romans 8:26

When your desperation brings you to the place where you have no words to express what is going on inside of you, take heart because God will meet you on the edge of that cliff and breathe His life into you as you exhale what needs to come out. I (Karen) know what it's like to sigh in desperation. I have walked through seasons of depression at different times in my life. I know it is slightly taboo to talk about walking through depression while in ministry; however, I have found that when you share your victories, you strengthen others to pursue God for victory as well. It's in the struggle that you become strong as you learn that your strength comes from God alone. When you abandon yourself to God, He renews your strength.

I am reminded of when my children were small and they would fall or scrape their knees. Oh, how the tears would flow. I would run to them and pick them up. For some reason at times I would blow on their little faces to calm them down. I am still not sure why I would do that. Maybe my mother did it to me, but for whatever reason it would calm them down. Do you think maybe God wants to do that for you and me? He is there when we fall, picking us up and breathing life into us.

I am truly blessed with an amazing, loving, fun, anointed family, but there have been times when the enemy has robbed me of my joy, peace, and purpose. It wasn't until I became uncomfortable with my condition that I decided to build an altar, where God's breath could flow freely through my heart, lungs, and soul. While our sighs are unintelligible to us, they are the very language of heaven. To God, they are prayers. We human beings can't interpret your sigh, but God can. If all you can do is sigh, then I believe you are on the verge of a supernatural encounter, and it's time for you to build a breathing room so God can breathe new life into you.

To truly appreciate what a breathing room is, we must go back to the Old Testament and understand God's desire for a personal relationship with His creation. In the beginning was the Word, and not only was the Word with God, but also it was God (John 1:1). Out of God, the Word, flowed the very breath of life. It was the breath of God that gave us life (Gen. 2:7).

In the Old Testament God's presence dwelt in the tent of meeting (Exod. 33). Then God sent His Son, and "the Word became flesh and dwelt among us" (John 1:14, MEV). The Greek word translated *dwelt* in John 1:14 can also mean "tabernacle." Through Jesus, the Word became flesh and "tabernacled" among us. We no longer have to go to a physical place (as in the Old Testament tabernacle) to encounter God. Christ now lives in us. The Old Testament tent of meeting is where God dwelt among man, and it was there that man brought his offering to God. In the New Testament, or under the new covenant, when it says Jesus "tabernacled" among us, it means He became the tabernacle, and not only that, but He also became the offering. Jesus came to earth in the flesh and then went back to God as the ultimate offering, allowing us to have direct access to God the Father.

On the cross, where Jesus loved us beyond human capability and gave His life for us, "Jesus called out with a loud voice, 'Father, into your hands I commit my spirit.' When he had said this, he breathed his last" (Luke 23:46). When Jesus breathed His last breath, He released the breath of God out into the world to dwell (tabernacle) within us so that we might have life and have it more abundantly (John 10:10). The enemy of our souls wants to steal the life, or breath, of God from us, but Jesus gave up His breath so that we might breathe it in and live. When Jesus declared on the cross, "It is finished," and breathed His last, He declared war on the enemy and victory for us! When we receive Jesus (the offering) as our Savior, we present ourselves back to God as living sacrifices.

Do you want a breathing room in your life? Do you want to create a place where the breath of God can reside? If so, we can turn to the Scriptures to find out how. The Bible mentions three distinct breathing rooms. In each of these places of encounter lives were altered. These three places also depict three different altar experiences. Let's look at them one by one.

The Breathing Room Where Life Is Restored

The first breathing room we are going to look at is found in 2 Kings 4:8–37, where we find the account of the Shunammite woman. This woman refused to give up and accept what the world declared about her son. Her son was dead to the natural eye, but she was determined to let God have the last word.

When we go back in the story, before her son died, we find this woman making room for the presence of God in her home. The Bible says the Shunammite woman recognized the presence of God on the prophet Elisha and built a room for him.

> "I'm certain," said the woman to her husband, "that this man who stops by with us all the time is a holy man of God. Why don't we add on a small room

upstairs and furnish it with a bed and desk, chair
and lamp, so that when he comes by he can stay
with us?"

—2 KINGS 4:9–10, THE MESSAGE

The Shunammite woman recognized that Elisha carried
the very breath of God in him and understood the value of
hosting the presence of God in her home. She wanted the
presence of God to be more than a guest in her home; she
wanted to create a room for it, so God's presence would
reside in her house. Through her actions she declared,
"God, You are welcome here!" Because of her generosity,
Elisha asked the woman if there was anything she needed
or desired. Even though she denied her need, God knew
what was in her heart. He knew she wanted a son to carry
on the family name and to receive the family inheritance.
Perhaps she had become so exhausted from travailing for
a son that she had given up on her dream. Yet when she
made room for the presence of God in her house, God
gave life to her dream.

Elisha prophesied that she would have a son, and indeed
at the appointed time she gave birth to a son, and he grew
into a young boy. Then one day the boy developed a massive headache and eventually died in the woman's arms. It
looked as if the dream had died again, but it was the enemy
trying to steal her seed. Please hear this: when the enemy
tries to convince you that it's time to walk away because the
promises of God are dead, that is the time to stand firm!
If when you find yourself in the midst of battle you have
already chosen to host the presence of God in your life,
then you have within you all you need to defeat the enemy.

When her son died in her arms, the Shunammite woman immediately took the boy to the room she had created to house the presence of God. Once there she called for Elisha to come and pray for him. Look at what she said when she contacted the prophet: "Did I ask for a son, master?" (2 Kings 4:28, THE MESSAGE). With this question she was declaring, "This is not my battle!" She knew the battle belonged to the Lord (2 Chron. 20:15).

She understood that the promises God gave her belonged to God; therefore she was able to walk in peace and boldness. We too must believe that God will do battle on our behalf. We must have an assurance that God is in control and will not leave us or forsake us.

Elisha went to the woman's home and upstairs to the room where the boy lay—the room of blessing the Shunammite woman created to house God's presence. Death wanted to get into that room of blessing to steal the woman's seed. But God would have the final say.

Elisha entered the room and saw the boy lying there dead on the bed. He proceeded to shut the door and pray; then he lay his body on the boy's body. He put his face to the boy's face, his eyes to the boy's eyes, his hands to the boy's hands, and as he did, the child's flesh warmed. And then we come to the really powerful part: "Then he got down...and bent over him; the boy sneezed seven times, and the boy opened his eyes" (2 Kings 4:35, MEV).

Let's pause for a moment here and consider two things from this passage. First, why did we need to know the boy sneezed seven times and then opened his eyes? The number seven represents completeness and perfection.[3] The child was experiencing the completeness and perfection of God in his physical body. Sneezing is one of the body's natural defense mechanisms. When we sneeze, a complex process takes place designed to rid the body of foreign invaders and to protect the lungs and other internal organs from contamination. A sneeze has a wind speed reaching ninety-three miles an hour! [4]

Those seven sneezes represented the power of the Holy Spirit, the wind of God. The Holy Spirit was blowing life back into the boy while simultaneously blowing out all the intruders that had come in and stolen life from him. This is the same breath of God mentioned in John 20:22 when Jesus "breathed on them [His disciples] and said to them, 'Receive the Holy Spirit'" (MEV).

Like the Shunammite woman, we need to build a room in our lives for the presence of God to dwell. We need to allow God to come in and clean out everything that is keeping us from living in the fullness of who God has called us to be. Our sneezes in this room will clear out our secret sin, our complacency, and our compromise so the breath of God can revive us.

In this Old Testament story it was a prophet of God who carried His presence. Under the new covenant we carry the presence of God. With that in mind, let's look at the second breathing room found in Scripture.

The Breathing Room Where God's Spirit Falls

After Jesus had risen from the grave and appeared to Mary Magdalene, Mary went to tell the disciples that she had seen the Lord.

On the evening of that first day of the week, when
the disciples were together, with the doors locked
for fear of the Jewish leaders, Jesus came and stood
among them and said, "Peace be with you!" After he
said this, he showed them his hands and side. The
disciples were overjoyed when they saw the Lord.

Again Jesus said, "Peace be with you! As the
Father has sent me, I am sending you."

—JOHN 20:19–21

The Scripture goes on to say that after He uttered those
words, Jesus breathed on them and said, "Receive the Holy
Spirit" (John 20:22, MEV). Isn't that amazing? In the disciples' worst moment, when they were full of fear and
despair, Jesus spoke peace and blew the breath of God on
them, saying in essence, "Receive My breath and inhale
the very Spirit of God into your life." This is what the Holy
Spirit does in desperate and weary people. The disciples
made a place for the Spirit of the living God to reside in
them, and when they did, He came and cleaned house. He
cleaned out the old man and filled the disciples with peace
and joy, empowering them to do what God was calling
them to do.

God does the same thing for us today that He did for
those disciples. When we create a place for Him in our
lives, He will always come and clean us up and empower
us for ministry. "Flesh gives birth to flesh, but the Spirit
gives birth to spirit" (John 3:6). The disciples were mere
flesh before Jesus gave them the power of the Holy Spirit.
Anything born of the flesh is flesh, but once Jesus says, "Be
filled with the Spirit," we are reborn by the Spirit.

The Greek word translated *Spirit* in John 3:6 is *pneuma,*

which can mean "breath" or "soul."[5] When you receive the Holy Spirit, you are being reborn by the breath of God put inside of you. Jesus told the disciples that He was sending them just as the Father had sent Him. Then He breathed on them. The moment Jesus breathed upon them, the disciples were resurrected. They received salvation as their spirits were awakened to the infilling of God's presence and His Spirit filled them with power! Jesus declared peace over them, then He empowered them and sent them out. They were commissioned and empowered for that assignment by the very breath of God.

What He did to the disciples He wants to do to you today. That moment with Jesus was an altar call for the disciples. That room became the altar where Jesus met and transformed them. Jesus breathed on them and sent them out as mighty men of God. We too are called to be mighty sons and daughters of God (1 John 3:1) because we were reborn by His Spirit (*pneuma*), the breath of God. We can face anything and everything the enemy brings our way because we are filled with God's very breath. This infilling did not stop with the disciples. It is available to us today if we will but make room for it. When we receive God's presence, we become the breathing room that the world so desperately needs. How, you ask? Let's look at how personal revival reflects this concept as we examine the third breathing room.

THE BREATHING ROOM THAT BIRTHS REVIVAL

The church was birthed in an upper room when God breathed on those few disciples who refused to leave until God showed up. (See Acts 1:1–5; 2.) Today God is still looking for those who will press in until they see victory and refuse to accept defeat. If we truly understand what took place through the death and resurrection of Christ, we will walk in freedom, resurrection power, and undying passion for Christ that the enemy cannot defeat. We will walk in purity with the very character of God manifesting in our lives, because the character of God is one of the gifts given to us at the cross, the altar where Jesus Christ became the sacrifice for our sin.

Jesus was the sacrificial Lamb. He took our place on the cross so we could represent Him in the world. That's why Paul could write, "I have been crucified with Christ and I no longer live, but Christ lives in me. The life I now live in the body, I live by faith in the Son of God, who loved me and gave himself for me" (Gal. 2:20). John 1:14 says that He dwelt among us, and we know that He also lives in us. That is why after the Day of Pentecost we find Peter saying, "For in him we live and move and have our being" (Acts 17:28).

We become the children of God when we accept Jesus as our Lord and Savior. We are adopted and grafted into Him. In the Upper Room the disciples were reborn by the Spirit (breath) of God and so experienced oneness with the Spirit. When you receive Christ and are filled with the Holy Spirit, your heart becomes the altar and the very throne room of God as He dwells in you. Then you become the breathing room, the breath of God, to a lost and dying world!

How then is it that we have this great gift of God's Spirit, His very breath living inside of us, yet we are not walking in power and authority and freedom and purpose? Why have we not seen true revival break out? Why is the altar of God not being restored in our lives and in our nation and world? The answer to these questions begins with each one of us. True revival begins when the children of God are restored! John 4:24 says, "God is Spirit, and those who worship Him must worship Him in spirit and truth" (MEV).

If God is the very breath of life, then His worshippers— those of us who are in Christ—must breathe in the breath and the truth of God. We must worship Him from somewhere deeper than our flesh. We must worship from the inner sanctuary of our hearts, which is the altar and throne room of our heavenly Father. It is there that we will be healed, delivered, restored, and revived. Revival will happen in the hearts of men and women who recognize the presence and breath of God and move aside to make room for God to inhabit their earthly vessels. It is inside of us that redemption, salvation, and the rebuilding of the altar take place.

Each one of us must work out our salvation with fear and trembling in the secret place, where the living, breathing presence of God is available to us. We must build a room in our hearts where the breath of God can reside. Romans 12:1 says, "Therefore, I urge you, brothers and sisters, in view of God's mercy, to offer your bodies as a living sacrifice, holy and pleasing to God—this is your true and proper worship." God showed His great mercy to us when His Word became flesh and dwelt among us. He became the offering for us so His breath could enter us and redeem us from the curse of sin, and our hearts could become His altar and throne room and we would no long be separated from Him.

Today, if you are weary and out of breath, struggling

to find the strength to run the race set before you; if your life is running on fumes and you are at the end of yourself, take heart! The end of yourself is the beginning of God and the place where life awaits you. The end of yourself is where you will find the altar, and God is waiting to meet you there. He is asking to meet with you and tabernacle with you today. He says, "Behold, I stand at the door, and knock: if any man hear my voice, and open the door, I will come in to him, and will sup with him, and he with me" (Rev. 3:20, KJV). I challenge you to open the door to your heart and allow God to breathe His Spirit into you. Allow God to reside in you and you in Him, and watch and see if your life isn't changed forever. Watch as you are empowered to live a life of purpose and passion as His presence in you begins to lead others to the altar of God.

CHAPTER 10

WE ARE REVIVAL!

E ARE MAKING a declaration today, and we pray that you will join us. We are declaring that *we are revival!*

Every believer is called to be the voice of God in the world. The Bible says, "We are therefore Christ's ambassadors, as though God were making his appeal through us" (2 Cor. 5:20). If we are God's mouthpieces, our words should spread revival to everyone we encounter. Our very lives should birth revival.

About a year ago Pat was walking through an airport on his way to speak at a conference when all of a sudden someone yelled, "Pat Schatzline!" He turned around, and a young woman in a military uniform ran up to him. She said she knew him from when He spoke at her church. She had recently been deployed and wanted him to pray for her and all those traveling with her to their deployment. The others in her group walked over to him and formed a circle around him; then Pat began to pray for their safety, protection, strength, and power to face the task ahead of them and the battles they would face. Pat became a flame of revival right there in that airport.

Just recently we were again at the church where this young woman had heard Pat preach, and her mom approached us and handed us a picture of her daughter. She asked us to pray for her daughter because she was facing a constant onslaught of spiritual and physical attacks from the enemy. We took that precious mom by the hand and prayed for her daughter. This young woman needed a revival in her spirit over a year ago, and now her precious mom needed a revival in her spirit as well to continue warring for her daughter's physical and spiritual protection. You see, there is a fire in us that those around us can feel, and it makes them say, "I need to be caught up and consumed in the source of strength and power they possess."

We are called to be "mobile breathing rooms." The atmosphere should shift when we walk into a room because when we enter, the Spirit of God comes in with us. We are atmosphere-changers, called to be light in the darkness.

When you possess God's Spirit in your being and you speak to others, God is making His appeal through you to the world. You are His voice and His hands and feet in this world. We see the fullness of this divine call in the life of Jesus. God spoke through the prophet Isaiah, saying of Jesus: "Here is my servant, whom I uphold, my chosen one in whom I delight; I will put my Spirit on him, and he will bring justice to the nations" (Isa. 42:1). God was saying He would put His breath, His *ruach*, which is Hebrew for "wind, breath, or spirit,"[1] upon His Son.

Seven hundred years later Jesus stepped into the synagogue in His hometown and was handed the scroll of the prophet Isaiah. He unfurled it, and God in the flesh made the same declaration to His people:

> The Spirit of the Lord is on me, because he has
> anointed me to proclaim good news to the poor. He
> has sent me to proclaim freedom for the prisoners and
> recovery of sight for the blind, to set the oppressed
> free, to proclaim the year of the Lord's favor.
>
> —LUKE 4:18–19

The powerful breath of God, capable of bringing forth life and resurrection, came to dwell among us. And when He left us to go sit at the right hand of the Father, Jesus put this same *ruach*, His holy breath, upon us! We are now His agents in the world, commissioned to take His very breath to the ends of the earth. We are temples of the Holy Spirit, who dwells in us. And we have Christ in us, the hope of glory (Col. 1:27)! We can live in a state of revival because our heart becomes the altar of God and the throne room for His presence when His Spirit is living in us. Jesus said, "On that day you will realize that I am in my Father, and you are in me, and I am in you" (John 14:20). The breath of the great I Am—the all-powerful, all-encompassing supreme authority—is upon us because Christ lives in us. His life in us gives us all we need to overcome the enemy, walk out our freedom, and become a breath of fresh air and hope to those we encounter each day.

It is crucial that we recognize who God has created us to be. We must know our identity in Christ because if we don't, Satan will give us a false identity. We tell each other and our children daily, "You are a champion, chosen by God to change the world. You are strong, brave, anointed, and loved. You are not a victim but an overcomer, empowered to defeat the enemy." There are days when we don't feel much like these words are true, but we choose to remind ourselves that God in us is all of these things and more. We must speak life and truth into ourselves and one another so we don't start living according to what the enemy tells us. When we speak life to ourselves, we prepare our hearts to expect a miracle. We begin to set the stage for a personal revival, which begins with our personal daily altar call.

We have already discussed the importance of creating a room for the Spirit (*pneuma*), or breath, of God. His very breath is what gives us life, power, and the authority to speak on His behalf and ultimately to overcome the world. Jesus said, "I have told you these things, so that in me you may have peace. In this world you will have trouble. But take heart! I have overcome the world" (John 16:33). The Shunammite woman built a room for the breath of God, and because of it her son received new breath in his lungs that resurrected his dead body. This "new breath" carried an authority that blew through his body, cleansing it of everything that was hindering the fullness of God's presence in the boy's life.

As believers we carry this same breath of authority from God to overcome this world. All we need to do is look to the life of Jesus. In Mark chapter 5 we find Jesus approaching the house of Jairus, one of the synagogue rulers. Jairus had come to Jesus to plead for healing for his dying daughter, but before Jesus could get to the child, she died. With everyone standing around mourning, Scripture tells us that the first thing Jesus did when He arrived at the house was to cast out unbelief.

> While Jesus was still speaking, some men came
> from the house of Jairus, the synagogue ruler. "Your

daughter is dead," they said. "Why bother the teacher anymore?" Overhearing what they said, Jesus told the synagogue ruler, "Don't be afraid: just believe."

—Mark 5:35–36

You see, although Jairus was a religious official, he had not yet grasped the fullness of God's love and power. Jesus saw this confusion and addressed it. Oh, how Jesus has had to confront the confusion and chaos in our lives at times. Sometimes in the midst of our disorder our trip to the altar will require us to go past our current trail of tears, through the crowds around us, and into the next phase of our journey with God. The first words out of Jesus's mouth—"Don't be afraid: just believe"—carried the power and authority to break through what had taken place in the flesh and usher in what was about to happen in the Spirit.

After putting the wailing mourners out of the house, Jesus got the little girl's parents and together they went to her. "The child is not dead but asleep," He said to them (Mark 5:39). Then, taking her by the hand, Jesus gave her a simple command: "'Talitha Koum!' (which means, 'Little girl, I say to you, get up!')" (Mark 5:41). Scripture says she immediately stood up and began to walk around.

Like this little girl whose breath had become so shallow it could no longer sustain her life, too many in the church today have become shallow breathers, barely living in the fullness of Christ while the world is dying around us. We often have failed to walk in the authority given to us because we were raised in religious settings that taught us we have no real spiritual authority. Maybe a pastor or church leader taught you that the authority to cast out demons, heal the sick, and walk in the power of God belonged to the church long ago and not to us today. But that's not true. That's not what the Scriptures say! Nowhere in Scripture does it say our commission and authority as believers in Jesus ended when the Bible was canonized. That's not the Word of God. The authority of Christ in us is available until Jesus returns in glory.

Like the daughter of Jairus, we need the hearth of our spirit to be reignited with the powerful, forceful breath of God so the fire that burns in our hearts will be stirred up and fanned back into flame. Jesus commanded Jairus's little girl to get up, and He is declaring to us, "Wake up!" He is telling us, "Wake up! Strengthen what remains and is about to die, for I have found your deeds unfinished in the sight of my God" (Rev. 3:2). When we wake up to our true authority-filled identity in Christ, we become alert, energetic, and alive again spiritually, with our eyes open to see what God has before us.

If we are to realize the fullness of who we are in Christ, we must live with the same kind of expectancy found in the woman with the issue of blood. This woman was reminded every day that she was unworthy to stand in public because her bleeding made her unclean in that day. The issue in her body was causing her to live in a constant state of embarrassment and shame. What she didn't know was that there was a war going on for her destiny.

There is a war going on for your destiny as well. The enemy knows that your tomorrow is at war with the issues of your today. Do you not realize that the attack you have been under was the enemy's way of keeping you from pursuing your purpose publicly? That's what he attempted to do with the woman with the issue of blood.

> A large crowd followed and pressed around him. And a woman was there who had been subject to bleeding for twelve years. She had suffered a great deal under the care of many doctors and had spent all she had, yet instead of getting better she grew worse. When she heard about Jesus, she came up behind him in the crowd and touched his cloak, because she thought, "If I just touch his clothes, I will be healed." Immediately her bleeding stopped and she felt in her body that she was freed from her suffering. At once Jesus realized that power had gone out from him. He turned around in the crowd and asked, "Who touched my clothes?"
>
> "You see the people crowding against you," his disciples answered, "and yet you can ask, 'Who touched me?'" But Jesus kept looking around to see who had done it. Then the woman, knowing what had happened to her, came and fell at his feet and, trembling with fear, told him the whole truth. He said to her, "Daughter, your faith has healed you. Go in peace and be freed from your suffering."
>
> —MARK 5:24–34

This woman was living in a prison called, "You're not worthy." She lived in a house of pain while looking out a window of shame. This is the same prison many of us live in every day, and it is what stops us from fulfilling our purpose and realizing that we are called to be revival. How can we become revival if we feel we are unworthy? The only way we will recognize our worth is to understand what has been freely given to us and placed inside of us. Jesus was about to show this woman that she was worthy of the Father's love, mercy, grace, and healing.

Something powerful happened that day to this woman. She received something powerful, and God wants us to receive the same thing. On that day the woman heard someone say, "Jesus is coming!" When she heard that, she knew she had to get to Jesus. So often we miss our breakthrough because we think we can't keep from being consumed by our issues. But not this woman. She determined that she would no longer live in bondage; she was ready for change.

This woman knew the Scriptures. She understood that Jesus was a kosher Jew and that underneath His robe He wore a prayer shawl, or a tallit, which represented His prayer life.[2] She knew that the very breath of God flowed through Him because of His prayer life. When she reached out to touch His garment, she was reaching out to touch the very breath of God! Jesus felt her touch because it was full of expectancy. Her expectancy is what we call faith. She expected to receive from Jesus. Much of the church today has lost its expectancy. We pray and we worship, and many "touch" Jesus, but this woman came expecting to *receive* Him.

When was the last time you went into your worship or prayer closet expecting to receive and be imbued with power? This reminds us of a recent incident when we were visiting a dear friend whose granddaughter was in the hospital fighting for her life. A horrible disease had struck the girl's body, and she was at the brink of death. We walked into that little hospital room to see the family, offer prayer, and war with them in the spirit. As we walked into that hospital room, we were hit with the powerful presence of a powerful, living, breathing God. He was in the very midst of them as they were crying out on behalf of that precious girl.

When we walked into that hospital room, over in the corner a powerful mother and grandmother were huddled together at their makeshift altar doing war in the heavenlies for their little girl. The presence of God overwhelmed us; the atmosphere was thick with the glory of God. We felt the power of God released in that room. It's a moment we will never forget. God began the process of healing and reviving that little girl in that moment.

In Mark 5 when Jesus asked, "Who touched my clothes?" it was because He felt power leave His body. He felt His own sustenance leave His body. The woman with the issue of blood had made a withdrawal from the very core of Jesus. It was an amazing moment because this had never happened before. Jesus began looking around for the courageous one in the crowd, the one who understood who He was and the power that He possessed. He was looking for the one who understood that revival was in Him, and if she reached for the power in Him, she would receive it and be revived.

There have been many times in our lives when we felt like this woman. We were at the end of ourselves and wanted to give up hope. We became desperate for change. Those times called for more than a memorized prayer or pulling a card out of a Scripture box. There are times in life when the enemy tries to overshadow you with a dark cloud of discouragement, depression, doom, gloom, and despair. During those times you will have to go beyond your comfort zone and passionately pursue your living Savior.

You must be willing to crawl through the crowd of the religious in order to deal with your issue. You must be willing to get down on scuffed-up knees, break your neatly manicured nails, embarrass your flesh, and get on some demons' nerves. We want you to make the forces of darkness tremble by waking up to the power that is in your reach as you stretch forth to touch God. Satan hates when you awaken to your ability to defeat him and his demons. For far too long he has been feasting on your flesh and tormenting you and your family. He does this because he knows that if he holds you back, you will never bring hope and life to others.

The woman didn't reach out to Jesus merely because of her sickness. She was reaching out to take back her authority so she could experience the resurrection power of Jesus. She needed to be revived from a dead state of being and brought back into the fullness of God. Because the woman was courageous enough to reach out and touch God and be revived, the people around her were awed by the power of God. This woman's pursuit of the presence of God (the altar) literally took holy breath away from Jesus. When we truly understand that revival is in us, we will receive our healing, our deliverance, our freedom, and our resurrection from the old life, and we will step into the new life and destiny God has planned for us.

When was the last time your pursuit of God's presence so captured His attention that it took His breath away?

POWER FROM ON HIGH

What Jesus gave the woman with the issue of blood He makes available to us. Power and strength flowed out from Jesus that day, and they still flow today if we will just ask. The Greek word for *power* is *dunamis*,[3] which is the root of the word *dynamite*.[4] When the woman with the issue of blood reached out and touched Jesus's tallit, which represented His prayer life, out of which flowed the breath of God, she was imbued with dynamite strength and courage to overcome that which had held her hostage for twelve long years. She became a living, breathing example of God's hope for humanity and the resurrection power of Christ. That same hope and resurrection power is still available today. The apostle Paul wrote, "To them God has chosen to make known among the Gentiles the glorious riches of this mystery, which is Christ in you, the hope of glory" (Col. 1:27). Revival lives inside of us. We are God's hope for humanity.

Our lives are living examples of what God can do through earthen vessels. I (Karen) shared in my book, *Dehydrated*, how God transformed a shy, insecure, fearful girl into a woman of power, purpose, and strength. It certainly did not happen overnight, but it was such a huge transformation that people who had not seen me in a while were shocked at the change. I'll never forget one summer about seven years ago when I met up with some lifelong friends for a weekend getaway. We had not seen each other in many, many years, and we wanted to just catch up on one another's lives. By the end of the weekend one of the women looked at me in amazement and said, "Who are you? You are not the shy, quiet, insecure girl I knew in high school. What happened to you?"

What happened was that broken, lost, fearful girl pushed through the chaos and the pain and found freedom when she reached out and touched her Savior. Jesus saw me in my despair and didn't leave me there, but He took me on a journey to find my purpose. Just as it was with the woman with the issue of blood, my pursuit of Jesus became hope and strength to others. They have said, "If you can reach out and touch Him and be so transformed, then I can move forward and touch Him as well." We become revival to those who need reviving.

The Welsh Revival, which took place from 1904 to 1905, was the largest Christian revival in Wales during the twentieth century. This mighty move of God was so dynamic, it triggered revivals in several other countries. Our dear friend Phillip Cameron once shared with us an account from the great Welsh Revival. The story begins with a man who took his family and traveled by train to experience what God was doing in Wales. He stepped off the train and saw a policeman standing nearby. Approaching the policeman, he asked to be pointed in the direction of Moriah Chapel, where the revival services were being held. Instead of pointing him to the chapel, the policeman simply tapped his chest and said, "Sir, the revival is in here!" [5]

You see, revival is not a location on a map but rather a place in our hearts. In the case of those dear friends we mentioned previously who were praying for their sick granddaughter, that hospital room became an altar as they decided to make room for the very breath of God to blow through that place. Our vision for a better tomorrow cannot be blinded by the spiritual sickness of our culture or our family today. It is the sudden awakening of our faith for something greater that leads us to experience the miracle of wholeness. We must purposefully make a room, a dwelling place in our hearts, to host the presence of God. In his letter to the church in Galatia the apostle Paul declared, "I have been crucified with Christ and I no longer live, but Christ lives in me. The life I now live in the body, I live by faith in the Son of God, who loved me and gave himself for me" (Gal. 2:20). That should be our prayer. On the cross Jesus switched places with us to make us His body in the earth. We must let Him *live* in us!

We are to be Christ to those who are lost and wandering hopelessly in a state of lethargy, dying for a breath of fresh air. We are to be the revival the world is looking for as we walk in the power and authority that comes from having Christ in us. If He truly is in us and we are in Him as He is in the Father, then there is no limit to what we can see take place on the earth. God is not concerned with our ministry titles or positions. He desires that we proclaim His name in all the earth. It's not about our platform or the next exciting program aimed at rallying the troops.

There has to come a time in your life when you realize that personal Pentecost precedes corporate Pentecost. Revival must begin in us first. There must be a personal awakening to who you are in Christ. You must experience a moment of awakening when you realize that you are the host of the glory of God.

Could it be that *we* are the change the world has been waiting to experience? Could it be that if we actually activated our faith, actually believed God's Word, that miracles would take place? Jesus told Nicodemus:

> Very truly I tell you, no one can enter the kingdom of God unless they are born of water and the Spirit. Flesh gives birth to flesh, but the Spirit gives birth to spirit. You should not be surprised at my saying, 'You must be born again.' The wind blows wherever

it pleases. You hear its sound, but you cannot tell where it comes from or where it is going. So it is with everyone born of the Spirit.

—JOHN 3:5–8

We are born of the Spirit and called to be the wind blowing throughout the land sparking revival fire! Christian leader Stephen Olford said, "Revival is ultimately Christ Himself, seen, felt, heard, living, active, moving in and through His body on earth."[6] How can that happen if we are not the hosts of revival? We are the physical hope that carries the spiritual fire of God in the altars of our hearts. G. Campbell Morgan, a close associate of Billy Graham's, once said, "We cannot organize revival, but we can set our sails to catch the wind from heaven when God chooses to blow upon His people once again."[7]

Did you catch that? Revival is not going to happen when a church leader decides to pencil it in as a calendar event. Revival will happen when we open our hearts, lay down our own ambitions, and put self-promotion aside, setting our hearts to catch the wind of heaven, which is the breath of God, as He blows upon His people again. Are you listening for the wind? Are you setting your sails in anticipation for Him to breathe on you again? Or are you like dry bones in the middle of a dry valley? Is God crying out to you as He did to Ezekiel to declare His living breath over your valley of dry bones? You may recall the passage from Ezekiel:

> The hand of the LORD was on me, and he brought me out by the Spirit of the LORD and set me in the middle of a valley; it was full of bones. He led me back and forth among them, and I saw a great many

bones on the floor of the valley, bones that were very dry. He asked me, "Son of man, can these bones live?" I said, "Sovereign LORD, you alone know." Then he said to me, "Prophesy to these bones and say to them, 'Dry bones, hear the word of the LORD! This is what the Sovereign LORD says to these bones: I will make breath enter you, and you will come to life. I will attach tendons to you and make flesh come upon you and cover you with skin; I will put breath in you, and you will come to life. Then you will know that I am the LORD.'"

So I prophesied as I was commanded. And as I was prophesying, there was a noise, a rattling sound, and the bones came together, bone to bone. I looked, and tendons and flesh appeared on them and skin covered them, but there was no breath in them. Then he said to me, "Prophesy to the breath; prophesy, son of man, and say to it, 'This is what the Sovereign LORD says: Come, breath, from the four winds and breathe into these slain, that they may live.'" So I prophesied as he commanded me, and breath entered them; they came to life and stood up on their feet—a vast army.

Then he said to me: "Son of man, these bones are the people of Israel. They say, 'Our bones are dried up and our hope is gone; we are cut off.' Therefore prophesy and say to them: 'This is what the Sovereign LORD says: My people, I am going to open your graves and bring you up from them; I will bring you back to the land of Israel. Then you, my people, will know that I am the LORD, when I open your graves and bring you up from them. I will put my Spirit in you and you will live, and I will settle you in your own land. Then you will know that I the Lord have spoken, and I have done it, declares the Lord.'"

—Ezekiel 37:1–14

While we are busy waiting on revival, God the Father is breathing down on us, waiting for us to become the revival.

Are you crying out for revival in your own life, in your family, or in the nation and world? Throughout the Scriptures, when God revived and resurrected someone, it opened the eyes of the community to His power. The woman at the well in John chapter 4 drank in the living water that is Jesus, and the eyes of her city were opened to the gospel. When Jesus healed Jairus's daughter, unbelief gave way to the reality of the kingdom of God. The story of the woman with the issue of blood demonstrates God's power and His great love and compassion.

A broken woman's faith awakened others. We must wake up too. We must stop settling for just enough and realize that He is more than enough. We must realize that we will never become revival until we stop looking out the window of pain and shame and open the front door, crawl out, and touch Jesus so we can experience our own freedom. Your act of faith will empower those around you. Walking out your faith and freedom will awaken others, including the next generation, to God's power.

When Jesus raised Lazarus from the dead, His very breath broke through the darkness of the grave and the stronghold of the enemy to bring forth resurrection. Jesus called Lazarus out of the tomb. (See John 11.) And He is calling us to declare the breath of life that resides in us through Christ Jesus over those around us who are spiritually dead and need to be revived (Ezek. 37:12). We are to speak life to the lost and dying and to resurrect and release His breath upon the earth again. When we step into the fullness of our God-given commission, the altar, or the place of the daily encounter, will be restored and we will see true revival in the land.

Are you tired of being a revival roadie? Are you ready to head to the upper room and receive the wind of His Spirit? Are you ready to build your personal altar to house the fire and presence of God? Romans 8:11 says, "And if the Spirit of him who raised Jesus from the dead is living in you, he who raised Christ from the dead will also give life to your mortal bodies because of his Spirit who lives in you." That means *all* authority given to Jesus is now given to us. How then is it that we are not standing up, looking in the mirror, and prophesying to ourselves, our families, our friends, our coworkers, and lost humanity, "*Live!*"

We are revival when our children wake up and need healing.

We are revival when we walk into work and pink slips are being handed out.

We are revival when our coworker finds out that she has cancer.

We are revival when we turn on the news and see there has been another terrorist attack.

We are revival when we meet someone who doesn't know Christ and is searching for answers.

We are revival when our children come home from school and tell us they have been attacked all day for standing up for truth.

We are revival when we go out to eat and the server needs to know that God loves him and knows his name.

We are revival when what is in us spills over to those around us and brings them joy in the midst of their sorrow. In every situation the Spirit of God living in us changes the atmosphere when we enter the room. We have the ability through Christ to bring peace, joy, freedom, and hope to others. I (Karen) am reminded of an incident one morning when I stopped by Walmart on my way home after dropping our daughter off at school. On this particular morning I had been praying and worshipping in the car because, quite frankly, I was tired after a busy season of traveling and speaking, and I needed a spiritual refreshing. I spent the entire drive just worshipping and praising God for all He had done in my life and in our family.

I have been known to frequent Walmart in the morning, and many of the cashiers recognize me. I have had regular conversations with many of them and have encouraged them on occasion. On this particular morning I wasn't paying attention and just randomly chose a checkout lane, not noticing who the cashier was. All of a sudden I heard someone shout, "Mrs. Schatzline! I need you to get over here in my checkout lane." It shocked me out of my daze, and I looked up to see the call coming from a precious lady I had talked to often on these morning trips to Walmart.

I quickly changed lanes and greeted her when I walked up. When I was in her lane, the woman said to me, "I needed a little bit of what you have this morning. You are always full of life and joy, and I need that today." *Wow.* I had not realized I had shown her that, but she noticed something beyond who I was; she noticed something

I possessed. Something inside me spoke to her need for something more than she had settled for. I was able to pray with her and speak life to her that morning. I had become the revival she was in need of. We need to realize that God wants to use us to speak to the areas that are spiritually dead in others and command them to live! We are to show people that God can resurrect and revive the areas they thought were dead and lost. They can live again and walk in freedom.

God told Ezekiel, "Prophesy to the breath; prophesy, son of man, and say to it, 'This is what the Sovereign LORD says: Come, breath, from the four winds and breathe into these slain, that they may live'" (Ezek. 37:9). Satan is busy stealing, killing, and destroying a generation. Are you going to sit this one out in the valley of dry bones, or are you going to take hold of the authority that has been given to you in Christ Jesus and declare revival over this generation?

With the breath given to us by the Spirit, we can prophesy the breath of life back into this generation and into the generations to come. When that happens, we will see the vast army of the remnant chosen by grace (Rom. 11:5–6) rise up and change the course of history.

We are called to be "mobile upper rooms," and the power in us should send the enemy into chaos. Demons should be jumping out windows when we walk into a room. You are the revival fire that God placed in the earth. Stop searching for a revival and accept the call to be the revival fire burning on the altar. If you build the altar and catch a flame upon it, people will come to see it burn, and they will be caught up in its warmth and will desire to burn as well. Let it be said of you, "I am aflame with the presence of God." Let your children see the flame burning in the early hours of the morning and as a lamp in the night. May our hearts burn within us (Luke 24:32).

Are you willing to be a tent dweller? Exodus 33:11 says, "The LORD would speak to Moses face to face, as one speaks to a friend. Then Moses would return to the camp, but his young aide Joshua son of Nun did not leave the tent." Moses returned to the camp, but Joshua stayed in the tent because everything within him was crying out to stay close to the presence of God. If you want to see revival in your personal life and in the land, then you must dwell in the tent when everyone else is walking away. Be a Joshua who stays in the presence of God even when it isn't required. Let your burning hunger for God become your source of life. When you allow God to be your source, He will stand with you in the dark times, guide you on the rough paths, and hold you when you have no strength. He is a personal God. He simply desires to abide in you and have you abide in Him (John 15:7).

Revival begins inside of you. *You* are revival! You become the awakening to those who are seeking hope. Your family, your friends, and the world are in desperate need of God's presence. So what are you waiting for? Stand and declare, "*I am revival!*"

CHAPTER 11

THE FAMINE AND THE HARVEST

THE PROPHET AMOS was an old shepherd farmer who lived at a time when people were satisfied with the status quo. He was a contemporary of many of the Old Testament's major prophets, who lived seven hundred years before Jesus. Amos was from the southern kingdom of Judah, but he preached to the northern kingdom. The northern kingdom had wealth and prosperity, which led them to become resistant to a holy lifestyle. The people had cast off all restraint and had no desire to make sacrifices to God. Their altars were broken down. Amos says they were like a basket of fruit that was easily destroyed. It was a dark time in the history of God's people, and Amos saw destruction coming. He prophesied a shaking in the land.

> "The days are coming," declares the Sovereign LORD, "when I will send a famine through the land—not a famine of food or a thirst for water, but a famine of hearing the words of the LORD."
>
> —AMOS 8:11

Does this sound familiar? It does to us. We are living in the same kind of desperate times in America. As the prophet Amos said, we are in a famine of hearing the word of the Lord. Once again God's people are in need of voices of truth to arise and declare His holy precepts over our land. The worst thing that could happen to our nation would be for God to turn us over to ourselves. I believe we are very close to that happening unless we are willing to let the famine compel us to build an altar once again.

Amos saw God standing at the altar bringing forth judgment:

> I saw the Lord standing by the altar, and he said: "Strike the tops of the pillars so that the thresholds shake. Bring them down on the heads of all the people; those who are left I will kill with the sword. Not one will get away, none will escape."
>
> —Amos 9:1

Because there was a famine in their hearts of the word of the Lord, calamity was coming. Satisfying their selfish desires had displaced their hunger for God. But God did not want to leave His people in this place of calamity. Through Amos, God spoke of the restoration of His house, the tabernacle of David. (As it happens, part of this word spoken through Amos was read in Israel's synagogues on the day in 1948 when they once again became a nation.[1])

> "In that day I will restore David's fallen shelter—I will repair its broken walls and restore its ruins—and will rebuild it as it used to be, so that they may possess the remnant of Edom and all the nations

that bear my name," declares the LORD, who will do these things.

"The days are coming," declares the LORD, "when the reaper will be overtaken by the plowman and the planter by the one treading grapes. New wine will drip from the mountains and flow from all the hills, and I will bring my people Israel back from exile.

"They will rebuild the ruined cities and live in them. They will plant vineyards and drink their wine; they will make gardens and eat their fruit. I will plant Israel in their own land, never again to be uprooted from the land I have given them," says the LORD your God.

—AMOS 9:11–15

In the darkest and most trying times God will show His greatness. Throughout history we see Him coming in power when the righteous cry out. In the worst moments of drought God's mighty arm will reach out for us, even though we tend to ignore Him in the good times and blame Him for the bad. Too often we build our theology out of our pain and fail to realize that God always has a good plan for us. In the midst of our drought He will call us to the altar. If we come, God will meet us there and bring the rain of His Holy Spirit. When His rain comes, it will water the fields so they fill with crops. And when the harvest is ready, God will raise up the workers to bring it into the storehouses of heaven.

This is a powerful biblical pattern revealed to us in Scripture that gives us strategy for the times we are in, and it consists of four stages. Stage one is drought, stage two is the altar, stage three is the rain, and stage four is the harvest.

I want to examine these four stages of God's powerful pattern for revival because I believe we can learn much from them that will help us in the times we are in now.

STAGE ONE: THE DROUGHT

America is in a drought of truth, and it is not a pretty picture. The reasons are many.

- We have embraced wrong over right.
- We have turned our back on Israel.
- We have embraced the lie that tolerance is only tolerance when it is celebrating perversion.
- Race profiteers are calling for and leading riots in the streets.
- The men and women who protect our streets now fear for their own lives.
- A fatherless generation has cast off all restraint.
- America is indebted financially for generations to come.
- Children are encouraged to choose their own gender.
- Women dressed in pink march in the streets by the thousands declaring their right to kill the unborn.
- Hollywood produces porn for all ages, and this nation continues to support the addiction.
- Politicians on all sides of the aisle spend their time bloviating instead of leading.

During times of crisis the church has almost always served as a moral compass. It was the church that stood up against abortion. It was the church that stood for biblical marriage. It was the church that fought against racism in many parts of America. It was the church in Germany, led by a man named Dietrich Bonhoffer, that fought Hitler and Nazi fascism. When German Christians were being told to only preach grace, not give altar calls, speak well of the government, keep their services short, and focus their efforts on helping the poor, Bonhoffer declared, "Cheap grace is the grace we bestow on ourselves. Cheap grace is the preaching of forgiveness without requiring repentance, baptism without church discipline, Communion without confession, absolution without personal confession. Cheap grace is grace without discipleship, grace without the cross, grace without Jesus Christ, living and incarnate." [2]

Let us also not forget that it was the church that decried injustice against Israel and helped them to become a nation in 1948. The church has been a moral compass many times, but today it seems Christian leaders take great pains to avoid controversy, even if that means not proclaiming God's Word. Over the last several years I have watched the social media accounts of prominent Christian leaders when the culture was burying God's truths. I had hoped that surely they would use their influence to bring some clarity to the culture's lies, that they would lay down their own agendas for the Lord's righteousness. But alas I heard crickets! For whatever reason, be it fear of retribution by the masses or the media, they remained silent in the face of the culture's lies. I must wonder aloud, "Do they not know they have been raised up for such a time as this?"

We must once again have leaders who will be stagehands for God, who are willing simply to open the curtain for Him and get out of the way.

We are living at a time when worship is loud, the lights are captivating, and the speakers are celebrated for their silence, all while truth is diminishing. Yet people are looking for answers. They are begging for help with their children. Mothers and fathers are hoping to find a sermon, a book, or a blog that will help them navigate what is swiftly becoming a godless America. We are in a drought of truth, and there is a desert of dehydrated believers all around us. This has created a famine in the land for the word of the Lord, and there is only one thing for us to do. We must have a spiritual and moral revolution to reawaken this once great nation.

We truly believe we hear the sound of rain coming. We both have had prophetic dreams of a giant wave headed toward America, which we shared in our books *Unqualified* and *Dehydrated*. Since then we have had many more dreams along the same line. It seems that the dreams have intensified as we see the coming persecution of the church. Yet we know that persecution is often the greatest antidote for a lethargic church. We must hurry and be about the business of winning souls and reviving the downcast because the fields are white unto harvest!

STAGE 2: THE ALTAR

Over and over in God's Word, when devastation and destruction overwhelm a nation or a kingdom, the people build an altar. Think of Nehemiah and Ezra. They joined forces to rebuild the altar in a time of despair. The boldness of Nehemiah and Ezra allowed Israel to once again meet at the altar of worship. Famine and the altar always work together, according to God's pattern and plan. We are living in a time of despair. God is looking for people who understand the cost of the altar.

He is looking for Ezras who will cry out:

> O my God, I am ashamed and embarrassed to lift up my face to You, my God, because our iniquities have expanded over our heads and our wrongdoing has grown up to the heavens.
> —EZRA 9:6, MEV

God desires Nehemiahs who will declare:

> I sat down and wept and mourned for days; and I was fasting and praying before the God of heaven. I said, "I beseech You, O LORD God of heaven, the great and awesome God, who preserves the covenant and lovingkindness for those who love Him and keep His commandments, let Your ear now be attentive and Your eyes open to hear the prayer of Your servant which I am praying before You now, day and night, on behalf of the sons of Israel Your servants, confessing the sins of the sons of Israel which we have sinned against You; I and my father's house have sinned.
> —NEHEMIAH 1:4–6, NASB

Who will rebuild God's holy altar amid the rubble of lost holiness and morality? Too many of today's leaders are so busy implementing the latest church-growth strategies that they are ignoring their own spiritual growth. The people of God must remember that they are His ambassadors called to deliver His message of hope and healing.

God will honor the altar you build in the midst of famine. He used Ezra and Nehemiah to restore His heritage and rebuild His altars, and He will do the same today for those who are willing to answer His call. And once you have built your altar and offered your sacrifice, God will bring His rain.

STAGE 3: THE RAIN

For three and a half years the prophet Elijah and all of Samaria were in a drought that had been sent from the Lord (1 Kings 17:1; 18:2). You will recall that Elijah was a prophet to the northern kingdom of Israel who announced to Ahab, king of the ten northern tribes of Israel, that a drought was coming upon the land because of the iniquity of the people and their king. This slide into the moral abyss began when King Ahab married the evil Jezebel, thus aligning himself and his kingdom with Jezebel's heathen gods. He went so far as to build an altar in Samaria to Baal and constructed an Asherah pole there also.

All of this angered God greatly. Scripture says, "Ahab...did more to provoke the LORD God of Israel to anger than all the kings of Israel who preceded him" (1 Kings 16:33, MEV). God's drought was a divine judgment on a nation that had turned away from Him to idolatry. Baal was believed to be the god of fertility and the lord of the rain clouds, yet when the drought hit the land, Baal could produce no rain. His altar was powerless, and God knew it. What ensued was a showdown between the false gods of the people of the northern kingdom and the one true God.

God instructed the prophet Elijah to rebuild His altar on Mount Carmel.

> Then Elijah said to all the people, "Come here to me." They came to him, and he repaired the altar of the LORD, which had been torn down.
>
> —1 KINGS 18:30

On the rebuilt altar Elijah assembled wood for the fire and then laid a sacrificial bull on the wood. He dug a trench around the altar, which Scripture says was "large enough to hold two seahs of seed" (1 Kings 18:32). Suffice it to say this was a large trench. Then Elijah instructed his helpers to fetch four large barrels of water and pour them over the bull and the wood on the altar. He did this to show that what was about to happen was from God, not some trick of man. Three times he ordered his helpers to pour water over the altar. Then he stepped back and prayed:

> "LORD, the God of Abraham, Isaac and Israel, let it be known today that you are God in Israel and that I am your servant and have done all these things at your command. Answer me, LORD, answer me, so these people will know that you, LORD, are God, and that you are turning their hearts back again."
>
> Then the fire of the LORD fell and burned up the sacrifice, the wood, the stones and the soil [called "dust" in other translations], and also licked up the water in the trench.
>
> When all the people saw this, they fell prostrate

and cried, "The LORD—he is God! The LORD—he is God!"

—1 KINGS 18:36–39

Did you notice what happened here? When Elijah rebuilt the altar, God came and received His sacrifice. But that's not all.

After God's fire fell on the altar, Elijah did something very important. He put his face to the ground and prayed, asking God to lift the covenant curse and bring rain (1 Kings 18:42). First Elijah built an altar and offered a sacrifice, and when God received His sacrifice, in thanksgiving Elijah bowed down in worship. As he knelt there with his face between his knees, in a posture of submission to God, he made his request known, asking God to lift the curse from the land and bring rain. Then, in faith, Elijah sent his servant to look for rain. Seven times he sent his servant, and each time the servant returned to say there was no rain—until that seventh time.

> On the seventh time, he reported, "There's a cloud as small as a man's hand coming from the sea." ... In a little while, the sky grew dark with clouds and wind, and there was a downpour.
>
> —1 KINGS 18:44–45, HCSB

Do you see what happened here? Once the false gods had been cast down by the power of God, then came the promise of rain (1 Kings 18:41). It all began with the altar. Samaria was starving. The people were desperate. Ahab, Jezebel, and the prophets of Baal had seduced them, and God had had enough. It was time for the heavens to open with fire and then rain! The altar brought an end to the drought.

If we are willing to build an altar, God will respond. Isaiah 43:18–19 is our promise: "Do not remember the former things nor consider the things of old. See, I will do a new thing, now it shall spring forth; shall you not be aware of it? I will even make a way in the wilderness, and rivers in the desert" (MEV). God will bring His fire and His rain if we will build the altar.

Right now God is bringing a great rain across the globe. Now more than ever we are hearing whispers of revival coming from the four corners of the earth. Many times these outbreaks of God go unnoticed because they are not induced by the Western church or led by a well-known person. Outbreaks of the Holy Spirit are taking place in house churches, caves, and hamlets where God is allowed to move at will and the people are begging for His presence.

The Word of God is banned in many of these places, but that has not stopped God. In fact, we hear almost weekly of miraculous and creative miracles taking place in countries where Christianity has been banned, but there is little mention of this in mainstream Christian churches in our nation. Many times the Christians in these foreign lands are in danger of losing their lives, but they count it all joy to be persecuted for His name's sake. Yet in America, where we are guaranteed freedom of religious expression, the church is often quiet. This is not because we do not have righteous and pure leaders, but rather because we have at times turned Christianity into a social club of "bought by the blood" saints who are discouraged from exhibiting exuberant praise for fear of being labeled "too radical" and losing their identity if they allow the Spirit to move in a way that elevates the voice of God over the voice of man. Nevertheless, we believe a growing majority of today's Spirit-led leaders are excited to see the saints arise and lead in exuberant worship. There is a paradigm shift taking place in the body of Christ. People are hungry for more of Jesus.

I have heard many fellow ministers ask why we must go overseas to see God perform miraculous signs and wonders. I can only conclude that perhaps at times God would rather move in a house church where worshippers are willing to praise Him even if it brings death than in a government-sanctioned house of worship where He is restricted by the "wisdom" touted in the latest church-growth conference. It is raining where God is banned and dry where His church is sanctioned.

This is not meant to be harsh, but rarely do we hear the words "Whoever has ears to hear, let them hear" uttered from pulpits today. Instead it is, "Let us not offend lest we lose our crowd and influence." It is time for believers—in the pulpit and the pews—to reject the seduction of man's Christianity, where we're more concerned about being seeker-sensitive than seeking God. If we are not careful, we will enter into another dark age, when the church is hidden from the world and irrelevant to its needs. The prophet Malachi decreed a powerful warning:

> "Oh, that one of you would shut the temple doors, so that you would not light useless fires on my altar! I

am not pleased with you," says the LORD Almighty,
"and I will accept no offering from your hands."
—MALACHI 1:10

We must check our spiritual pulse and ask ourselves if
God is pleased with what we are doing. Jesus gave a stern
warning in Revelation 2:4–5: "But you walked away from
your first love—why? What's going on with you, anyway?
Do you have any idea how far you've fallen? A Lucifer fall!"
(THE MESSAGE).

We have allowed the winnowing fork to become dull
and are attempting to make the narrow gate wide. The
propagation of a powerless message is a scheme of the
enemy designed to seduce Christ's bride into an adul-
terous relationship with the world. General William Booth,
founder of The Salvation Army, prophesied over 130 years
ago, "The chief danger of the 20th century will be religion
without the Holy Spirit, Christianity without Christ, forgiveness without repentance, salvation without regenera-
tion, politics without God, and heaven without hell."[3] It is
past time to wake up. The harvest is coming. "Let us not
become weary in doing good, for at the proper time we
will reap a harvest if we do not give up" (Gal. 6:9). This
could be the finest hour of the church if we wake up! Now
is our moment!

We must answer the Revelation 22:17 call to come to
Jesus and drink freely! The bride of Christ must stand
firm and take the microphone from the enemy. Our voice
cannot be muted. The church is the bloodline of this
nation. Now more than ever we must rebuild the broken-
down altars. We must grab a hammer called "truth" and

a nail called "the anointing" and once again experience freedom at a holy altar. "Blow the trumpet in Zion, declare a holy fast, call a sacred assembly" (Joel 2:15)! The church must be the counterculture voice that restores the nation. Do not worry about the retribution of man. You have God on your side! We are experiencing famine in our land. Now is the time to rebuild the altar and pray for the rain.

> Ask rain from the LORD at the time of the spring rain—the LORD who makes the storm clouds; and He will give them showers of rain, vegetation in the field to each man.
> —ZECHARIAH 10:1, NASB

> Be glad, people of Zion, rejoice in the LORD your God, for he has given you the autumn rains because he is faithful. He sends you abundant showers, both autumn and spring rains, as before.
> —JOEL 2:23

We believe we are close to the next mighty outpouring of God. We see signs of this every day. We have watched as thousands have run to the altar crying out to God. Every week it seems a lone soul will move toward the altar and start the flood that breaks open the gate. At the altar many times they are sobbing or weeping as the weight of their sin and sorrow overtakes them. They often do not wait for the invitation; they simply come and heaven rejoices as they climb upon the altar.

The Bible says that all of the martyrs in heaven live under the altar.

> When he opened the fifth seal, I saw under the altar the souls of those who had been slain because of the word of God and the testimony they had maintained. They called out in a loud voice, "How long, Sovereign Lord, holy and true, until you judge the inhabitants of the earth and avenge our blood?"
>
> —REVELATION 6:9–10

Perhaps they are under the altar because they want to hear the wails of the lost being set free. After all, this is what they gave their lives for—for the sinner to be saved. They are avenged because the altar is the place of restoration for the soul. That is a true *selah* notion, something to pause and think on!

As I have studied the progression of revival from the First Great Awakening to the most recent revivals of this century, I see five things that seem to happen when a move of God hits a morally depleted sleeping church. First, the sinner begins to hate the sin in their own life and in the culture. Next, they begin to preach the full gospel of Jesus with the demonstration of God's power. Then they develop a deep burden for others and the lost-ness of man, which then leads them to pray and fast as never before. And when all of this is fully formed in them, they become completely obedient to God. This is a picture of what it takes for the kingdom of God to advance. And this is what it looks like for things to be "on earth as it is in heaven" (Matt. 6:10).

Rain produces crops, and crops require laborers. When the rain of God brings a wave of repentance, a rich crop springs up upon the land (Amos 9:13). There is a healing coming to the land. "If my people, who are called by my name, will humble themselves and pray and seek my face and turn from their wicked ways, then I will hear from heaven, and I will forgive their sin and will heal their land" (2 Chron. 7:14). When this rich harvest comes, all must put their hand to the plow, lest the crops rot in the field.

STAGE 4: THE HARVEST

We can clearly see the pattern in 1 Kings 18 of the famine, the altar, and the rain. Then after the rain comes the harvest, which means it is time for the harvesters to come forth. In 1 Kings 19 the people had returned to the altar and God had sent the rain. Now God was ready to release a mouthpiece who would call the people back to righteousness. We might assume Elijah was that man, but God had another plan. He wanted the revival to last, so He spoke to Elijah to anoint someone who would pick up the mantle and continue to run with it after he was gone.

It is not a coincidence that Elisha was in a field farming when Elijah found him. Elisha was a harvester. He was doing in the natural what God was calling him to in the spirit. He was called to harvest souls, to call the people back to righteousness. He had been working steadily, not fully realizing what God had planned for him. Maybe he had dreams of being used of God and wondered if that dream would ever come to pass. We don't know. The Scriptures don't say. But we see Elisha faithfully harvesting seed in the natural until the prophet of God stopped by one day.

So Elijah went from there and found Elisha son of Shaphat. He was plowing with twelve yoke of oxen,

and he himself was driving the twelfth pair. Elijah
went up to him and threw his cloak around him.
—1 Kings 19:19

Elisha was a harvester, and he represented what we must
have come forth once the altar has been rebuilt—those
who will bring in the harvest of souls and call people
back to righteousness. Elisha was in the midst of plowing
when his work was interrupted as Elijah's cloak fell on
his shoulders. This was a sign, a call of God for Elisha to
leave everything behind for what lay ahead. The altar had
been built, the rain had come, and now it was time for the
harvest. Elisha the harvester would pick up the mantle of
Elijah and go into the harvest fields, walking in double the
anointing of Elijah.

Before Elisha was released, he would watch as Elijah
performed miracles under the mighty hand of God. He
would make sure the old prophet was always in need
of nothing. He not only walked beside him, but he also
learned from him. Then eventually his time would come
to pick up the mantle (2 Kings 2:13). I truly believe that
the greatest need we have in the body of Christ is mantle
releasers and mantle catchers—those who are willing to
pour into the next generation of leaders and those who are
willing to wait their turn to be released and stay faithful
to the vision in the meantime. Many times the mantle
catchers may think their time will never come, but it will
when the timing is right.

Is God calling you to bring in the harvest? Is He calling
you to catch the mantle of this generation of altar builders
and bring in the souls just waiting to be reached after

God sends the rains of revival? Maybe this is your passion, and you've been in a waiting season for what seemed like forever. Know this: you have been hidden for a reason and prepared for a purpose. Remember the words of the apostle Paul: "Let us not become weary in doing good, for at the proper time we will reap a harvest if we do not give up" (Gal. 6:9). You may think you have been forgotten, but harvest time is coming soon, and the body of Christ will need harvesters. Jesus spoke many times of this need.

> Don't you have a saying, "It's still four months until harvest"? I tell you, open your eyes and look at the fields! They are ripe for harvest.
> —John 4:35

> The harvest is plentiful, but the workers are few. Ask the Lord of the harvest, therefore, to send out workers into his harvest field.
> —Luke 10:2

The move of God will not reach its fullness without those who will take their place in the kingdom and bring in the harvest. The body of Christ needs disciplers and soul winners in the last days. We need those who will go into foreign lands and lay down their lives for the cause of Christ. After the drought comes the altar, then the rain, then the harvest—"for ground that drinks the rain which often falls on it and brings forth vegetation useful to those for whose sake it is also tilled, receives a blessing from God" (Heb. 6:7, NASB).

We have been given a promise that we will be used mightily by God in these last days. Jesus said, "Very truly

I tell you, whoever believes in me will do the works I have been doing, and they will do even greater things than these, because I am going to the Father" (John 14:12). As we bring in the harvest, we can be confident in the One who sends us, for as the psalmist said, "I have never seen the righteous forsaken or their children begging bread" (Ps. 37:25).

Are you willing to be like Elisha and take up your mantle? Heaven is watching from the grandstands to see what your response will be. God is looking for His people to rise up! He is looking for those who are without an agenda because the coming days will not be easy for the church. Persecution is coming. But we are to take heart because all of this is a setup for revival. Persecution always precedes a move of God. If we will follow the road from famine to the altar, wait for the rain, and bring in the harvest, God's purposes will be accomplished in our hearts and in the world.

CHAPTER 12

IT'S TIME TO BURN FOR HIM!

T HE BIBLE SAYS that Elisha burned the plow, and then he set out to follow Elijah and became his servant (1 Kings 19:21). I imagine that fire burned everyone who stopped to watch it. "What is this man doing?" the people must have wondered. Farming was Elisha's livelihood, and now he was burning his plow. Was he crazy? No! He was letting the world know that he was giving himself to setting things on fire for God!

The world is not looking for a space heater with which to warm their toes, but rather a bonfire that warms their inner man. We must be God's embers that restart the brushfire of revival. Hebrews 12:28–29 tells us, "Therefore, since we are receiving a kingdom that cannot be moved, let us be gracious, by which we may serve God acceptably with reverence and godly fear. For our God is a consuming fire" (MEV).

God has called us to burn for Him! Will you? This will require that our lamps stay trimmed and burning in expectation of His return (Matt. 25:10). It is time to be a spectacle for God. John Wesley once said, "Catch on fire and others will love to come watch you burn."[1] We are called to be the burning ones! The world is looking for a light that will shine in the darkness. Jesus said, "Neither do men light a candle and put it under a basket, but on a candlestick. And it gives light to all who are in the house" (Matt. 5:15, MEV). We must let our light shine, and we must allow His fire to burn up everything that isn't like Him.

When we meet God at the altar, the fire of God we encounter there is all-consuming. When Elijah confronted the prophets of Baal on Mount Carmel, the Bible says the fire fell and burned up everything—including the dust on the altar (1 Kings 18:38)! When God's fire falls on us, it will consume everything, including the areas in our life where dust has accumulated. The Bible speaks of the refiner's fire in Malachi 3:2. This is a fire that is hotter than any other fire. It has the ability to burn away impurities and bring forth uncorrupted gold. The fire of God does the same thing in us. Job said, "But he knows where I am going. And when he tests me, I will come out as pure as gold" (Job 23:10, NLT). On the altar God will purify you and prepare you to shine for Him!

If you long to burn for God, you must decide that sin is offensive and that you will march toward holiness! It is time for us to awaken to the call of God. It is time for us to draw a line in the dust of our lives. The kingdom of God is not about words but the demonstration of His power (1 Cor. 4:20)! How long will we waver between two opinions? The shame Jesus suffered on the cross must be met with the hunger of the righteous and the redeemed.

Many of us in the church have prayed for revival, but

we often do not realize that with revival comes Satan's attack. The New Testament church must rise to the occasion and stand firm! Yet with increased wickedness in the land also comes increased grace to stand against it! (See Romans 5:20.) Will history declare, "This was the church's finest hour"? Or will the world only remember what the media and the anti-church culture has said of us—that the church was filled with bloated, egotistical, money-hungry, self-righteous people who professed a faith they failed to demonstrate?

May the latter never be so! May we always be known as those who walked in love, truth, power, and freedom. Jesus told us how we should be remembered: "A new command I give you: Love one another. As I have loved you, so you must love one another. By this everyone will know that you are my disciples, if you love one another" (John 13:34–35). Let us make it our mission to keep one hand on the cross and the other snatching the lost from the fire so the church will never slide into oblivion! We must keep marching toward the gates of hell. We must keep pursuing the lost. We must never, ever give up on the least of these. We are called to stand between the living and the dead and break the curses (Num. 16:48). The epitaph of today's church shall never read, "The once-lost-and-now-found forgot to give away the truth that delivered them from darkness; thus their light no longer burns in a dark world."

May the church never have a tombstone, but rather always burn a neon sign that lights up the caverns of darkness, the foggy streets of eternity, the forests of fear, and the oceans of obscurity. Its light should shine brightly, declaring, "Jesus Christ is Lord, and He came to seek and to save that which was lost."

This is the hour in which men must once again crawl to the altar of repentance and burn with a fire that cannot be extinguished. May eternity say of us, "These were the ones who grabbed hold of the altar and held on to that which released them from the weight of their sin and pain! These were the ones who with unabated breath labored in the fields that were white unto harvest."

Let us now make ready, for the battle is beginning and the salute of the righteous must be to welcome the King of kings as we wave good-bye to the opinions of finite man. This is the hour in which our hearts will be judged not by our works but by whether we truly understand that we possess Christ in us, the hope of glory!

Your voice matters now more than ever. Will you speak up? Dare we say to our kids that our nation was destroyed because we who called ourselves believers in Jesus were not willing to pay the price for speaking up? Will they look back and declare that we were loud for the wrong reasons and cowered in the harvest season? We must speak up before we miss our moment. Let history declare that we were those who chose holiness over heathenism and purpose over procrastination. This is our now! We must rise up and lead a Holy Spirit revolution.

This brings to mind the apostle Paul's mandate to Timothy, when he said:

> You take over. I'm about to die, my life an offering
> on God's altar. This is the only race worth running.
> I've run hard right to the finish, believed all the way.

All that's left now is the shouting—God's applause!
Depend on it, he's an honest judge. He'll do right not
only by me, but by everyone eager for his coming.
—2 TIMOTHY 4:6–8, THE MESSAGE

Let us make our lives offerings on God's altar.

The church must once again be the moral compass of our nation. The world is awaiting the messengers of God's light and love, who are ready to battle hell for our children, the church, and our lost companions and future compatriots! Let us join forces and march where men rarely glance, love where demons have taken dominion, and declare truth where the righteous have been mute! The flame of revival that cannot be extinguished will burn ever so brightly when we put our lives on the altar, allowing our flesh to be burned up by His glory! We must never doubt our calling. We do not possess that right. We are the fellowship of "the altared"!

We'd like to end this journey with a favorite quote from a man who led a remnant movement for God nearly 150 years ago:

> "Not called!" did you say?
> "Not heard the call," I think you should say.
> Put your ear down to the Bible, and hear Him bid you go and pull sinners out of the fire of sin. Put your ear down to the burdened, agonized heart of humanity, and listen to its pitiful wail for help. Go stand by the gates of hell, and hear the damned entreat you to go to their father's house and bid their brothers and sisters and servants and masters not to come there. Then look Christ in the face—whose

mercy you have professed to obey—and tell Him whether you will join heart and soul and body and circumstances in the march to publish His mercy to the world.[2]

—William Booth
Founder, The Salvation Army

God has created you for such a time as this, and it is time for us all to go public. We represent the altar to lost humanity. We are ambassadors of Christ. If we are faithful to seek God at the altar, together we will see a harvest like never before. So get out your hammer and nails. It's time to rebuild the altar!

NOTES

FOREWORD BY DR. MARK SPITSBERGEN

1.   "Evan Roberts Testimony—1878–1951," The Revival Library, accessed February 16, 2017, http://www.revival-library .org/index.php/pensketches-menu/evangelical-revivalists/roberts -evan-his-own-testimony.

INTRODUCTION
CALLING THE ALTARED!

1.   Paul Owens, in communication with the author.

CHAPTER 1
MEET ME AT THE ALTAR!

1.   Oswald Chambers, "Yesterday," December 31, My Utmost for His Highest, accessed February 14, 2017, https:// utmost.org/yesterday/.

2.   Rodney Howard-Browne, in communication with the author.

3.   "How BIG was Noah's Ark?," The Bible Study Site, accessed March 9, 2017, http://www.biblestudy.org/basicart /was-noah-ark-big-enough-to-hold-all-animals.html.

4.   "Ancient Altars," Bible History Online, accessed February 14, 2017, http://www.bible-history.com/biblestudy/altars .html.

5.   Blue Letter Bible, s.v. "ga'al," accessed March 9, 2017, https://www.blueletterbible.org/lang/lexicon/lexicon.cfm ?t=kjv&strongs=h1350.

6.   The prophet Micah foretold that it would happen in a tiny town called Bethlehem in Micah 5:2.

7.   "The Books of the Bible," Blue Letter Bible, accessed March 9, 2017, https://www.blueletterbible.org/study/misc /66books.cfm.

8.   Grant McClung, "We Have an Altar (Hebrews 13:10)," Enrichment Journal, accessed February 14, 2017, http:// enrichmentjournal.ag.org/200903/200903_000_Altar.cfm.

9.   Ibid.

CHAPTER 2
WHERE HAVE THE ALTARS GONE?

1.   Portions of this chapter were drawn from Patrick Schatzline, "The Problem With Being Relevant," Charismamag.com, September 2, 2014, accessed February 14, 2017, http://www.charismamag.com/spirit/church-ministry/19759-the-problem-with-being-relevant.

2.   "Charles Spurgeon on Discernment," Apologetics 315, accessed March 9, 2017, http://www.apologetics315.com/2013/02/charles-spurgeon-on-discernment.html.

3.   "Leonard Ravenhill Quotes," Good Reads, accessed March 9, 2017, http://www.goodreads.com/quotes/671830-the-greatest-miracle-that-god-can-do-today-is-to.

CHAPTER 3
BURNING HEARTS AND BROKEN BREAD

1.   Jack Hayford, "A Time of Altars," Jack Hayford Ministries, accessed March 10, 2017, http://www.jackhayford.org/teaching/articles/a-time-of-altars/.

2.   Ibid.

3.   "St. Cleopas of Emmaus," The New Theological Movement, May 7, 2011, accessed March 10, 2017, http://newtheologicalmovement.blogspot.com/2011/05/st-cleopas-of-emmaus-martyr-brother-of.html.

4.   Jewish Encyclopedia, s.v. "Emmaus," accessed March 10, 2017, http://www.jewishencyclopedia.com/articles/5738-emmaus.

5.   Sermons and Biblical Studies, s.v. "feelings," accessed March 10, 2017, http://www.biblia.work/sermons/feelings-2/.

6.   C. S. Lewis, *The World's Last Night and Other Essays* (New York: Houghton Mifflin Harcourt, 2002), 9, viewed at Google Books.

7.   As quoted by Lisa Bevere, *Girls With Swords* (Colorado Springs, CO: Multnomah, 2013), 209; also viewed at Sermon-Index.net, "William Booth Quote 4," accessed February 16, 2017, http://www.sermonindex.net/modules/myalbum/photo.php?lid=3241.

8.   Charles Spurgeon, "David's Prayer in the Cave," *The Biblical Illustrator*, accessed March 10, 2017, http://biblehub.com /sermons/pub/david's_prayer_in_the_cave.htm.

CHAPTER 4
TIE ME TO THE ALTAR

1.   Jonathan Cahn, "The First of Loves," July 7, 2014, accessed March 10, 2017, http://the-hand-of-god.com/sapphires /2014/1/6/the-first-of-loves.

2.   Philip O'Dowd, "The Back of the Bulletin: Abraham," Philip O'Dowd.com, accessed March 10, 2017, http://philip-o -dowd.com/web2/bob/0506b/Lent2b1.pdf.

3.   "16.3.1. Abraham Offers Isaac," Bible Study Tools, accessed March 10, 2017, http://www.biblestudytools.com/commentaries /revelation/related-topics/abraham-offers-isaac.html.

4.   Dave Fidlin, "Billy Graham Quotes on Life: 11 Memorable Statements From Evangelical Christian," Newsmax, December 26, 2014, accessed March 10, 2017, http://www.news max.com/FastFeatures/billy-graham-quotes-life-memorable /2014/12/26/id/615148/.

5.   Oswald Chambers, "A Bondservant of Jesus," My Utmost for His Highest, November 3, accessed March 10, 2017, https:// utmost.org/a-bondservant-of-jesus.

CHAPTER 5
AFTER THE ALTAR COMES THE WHISPER

1.   Blue Letter Bible, s.v. "'*Eliyah*," accessed March 10, 2017, https://www.blueletterbible.org/lang/Lexicon/Lexicon.cfm ?strongs=H452&t=KJV.

2.   Pat Schatzline, *I Am Remnant* (Lake Mary, FL: Charisma House, 2014), 168–169.

3.   Chris Moen, "Jeremiah the Prophet," Life, Hope & Truth, accessed March 10, 2017, https://lifehopeandtruth.com/prophecy /prophets/prophets-of-the-bible/jeremiah-the-prophet/.

4.   This statement was popularized by evangelist T. L. Osborn.

5.   Charles Spurgeon, "David's Prayer in the Cave," Christian Classics Ethereal Library, accessed March 10, 2017, http://www.ccel.org/ccel/spurgeon/sermons38.xlvi.html.

6.   Ibid.

7.   Ibid.

8.   Ibid.

9.   Ibid.

10.   Ibid.

11.   Ibid.

Chapter 6
Dismantling the Altar of Offense

1.   Cambridge Dictionary, s.v. "friendly fire," accessed March 10, 2017, http://dictionary.cambridge.org/us/dictionary/english/friendly-fire.

2.   As quoted in Bill Wilson, "Don't Go to Hell Over a Mystery," *The Metro Report*, December 1993.

3.   Blue Letter Bible, s.v. *"skandalizo,"* accessed March 10, 2017, https://www.blueletterbible.org/lang/lexicon/lexicon.cfm?t=kjv&strongs=g4624.

4.   "The Extent of Fatherlessness," National Center for Fathering, accessed March 10, 2017, http://www.fathers.com/statistics-and-research/the-extent-of-fatherlessness/.

5.   Louis Jacobson, "CNN's Don Lemon Says More Than 72 percent of African-American Births Are Out of Wedlock," Politifact, July 29, 2013, accessed March 10, 2017, http://www.politifact.com/truth-o-meter/statements/2013/jul/29/don-lemon/cnns-don-lemon-says-more-72-percent-african-americ/; NewsOne Staff, "72 Percent of Black Kids Raised by Single Parent, 25% Overall in U.S.," accessed March 22, 2017, https://newsone.com/1195075/children-single-parents-u-s-american/.

6.   Chris Summers, "'Too often, we judge other groups by their worst examples while judging ourselves by our best intentions': Moving Quote by George W. Bush at Dallas Police Memorial Inspires America," Daily Mail, July 13, 2016, accessed March 10, 2017, http://www.dailymail.co.uk/news/article-3687974/Too-judge-groups-worst-examples-judging-best-intentions-Moving-quote-George-W-Bush-Dallas-police-memorial-inspires-America.html.

7.   Blue Letter Bible, s.v. "*Yowceph*," accessed March 10, 2017, https://www.blueletterbible.org/lang/Lexicon/Lexicon .cfm?strongs=H3130&t=KJV.

8.   Herbert Lockyer, *All the Women of the Bible* (Grand Rapids, MI: Zondervan, 1988), "Jochebed," accessed March 10, 2017, https://www.biblegateway.com/resources/all-women-bible /Jochebed.

9.   C. S. Lewis Institute, "The Necessity of Forgiveness," January 2007, accessed March 10, 2017, http://www.cslewis institute.org/webfm_send/103.

Chapter 7
When Tomorrow Becomes Today

1.   Blue Letter Bible, s.v. "Bethesda," accessed March 9, 2017, https://www.blueletterbible.org/lang/Lexicon/Lexicon.cfm ?strongs=G964&t=KJV.

2.   Jared Kern, "Bethel, Bethlehem, and Bethesda," 2 or 3 Gathered in His Name, accessed March 9, 2017, http://2or3 .co/2013/03/25/bethel-bethlehem-and-bethesda/; see also Wayne Blank, "The House of Mercy," Daily Bible Study, accessed March 9, 2017, http://www.keyway.ca/htm2010/20100217.htm.

3.   "Chapter 5: Numbers 31-40," Kingdom Ministries, accessed March 9, 2017, http://gods-kingdom-ministries.net /teachings/books/the-biblical-meaning-of-numbers/chapter-5 -numbers-31-40/.

4.   "God Counts," Straight Talk About God, accessed March 9, 2017, http://asis.com/users/stag/godcount.html.

Chapter 8
Rebuilding the Altar in Your Home

1.   Ken Bailey, "Meaning of Prodigal Son Parable," eProdi-gals.com, March 9, 2017, http://www.eprodigals.com/The -Prodigal-Son/The-Prodigal-Son-God-Runs.html; Matthew Wil-liams, "The Prodigal Son's Father Shouldn't Have Run!," *Biola* magazine, Summer 2010, http://magazine.biola.edu/article/10 -summer/the-prodigal-sons-father-shouldnt-have-run/.

2.   Joseph S. Exell, "Commentary on 2 Kings 4:4," *The Bib-lical Illustrator*, accessed March 9, 2017, http://www.studylight

.org/commentaries/tbi/2-kings-4.html; see also Jim Cole-Rous, "The Creditor and God's Deliverance," Global Christian Center, accessed March 9, 2017, http://globalchristiancenter.com/christian-living/lesser-known-bible-people/31412-the-creditor-and-gods-deliverance.

3. Blue Letter Bible, s.v. "*nashah*," accessed March 9, 2017, https://www.blueletterbible.org/lang/Lexicon/Lexicon.cfm?strongs=H5383&t=KJV.

4. Bible Hub, s.v. "fatness," accessed March 9, 2017, http://biblehub.com/topical/f/fatness.htm.

5. Exell, "Commentary on 2 Kings 4:4"; see also Cole-Rous, "The Creditor and God's Deliverance."

CHAPTER 9
ARE YOU OUT OF BREATH?

1. *Oxford Living Dictionaries*, s.v. "revival," accessed March 9, 2017, https://en.oxforddictionaries.com/definition/revival.

2. As quoted in Billy Graham, *Hope for the Troubled Heart: Finding God in the Midst of Pain* (Nashville, TN: Thomas Nelson, 1991), viewed at Google Books.

3. "The Meaning of Numbers: The Number 7," BibleStudy.org, accessed March 9, 2017, http://www.biblestudy.org/bibleref/meaning-of-numbers-in-bible/7.html.

4. Elizabeth Palermo, "Why Do We Sneeze?" Live Science, March 25, 2014, accessed March 9, 2017, http://www.livescience.com/44362-why-do-we-sneeze.html.

5. Blue Letter Bible, s.v. "*pneuma*," accessed March 9, 2017, https://www.blueletterbible.org/lang/Lexicon/Lexicon.cfm?strongs=G4151&t=KJV.

CHAPTER 10
WE ARE REVIVAL!

1. Bible Hub, s.v. "*ruach*," accessed March 9, 2017, http://biblehub.com/hebrew/7307.htm.

2. Charlie Kluge, *The Tallit* (Lake Mary, FL: Charisma House, 2016).

3. Bible Hub, s.v. "*dunamis*," accessed March 9, 2017, http://biblehub.com/greek/1411.htm.

4.   GotQuestions.org, "What is the meaning of the Greek word *dunamis* in the Bible?," accessed March 9, 2017, https://www.gotquestions.org/dunamis-meaning.html.

5.   Phillip Cameron, in communication with the author, January 2017.

6.   SermonIndex, Stephen Olford Quote, accessed March 9, 2017, http://www.sermonindex.net/modules/myalbum/photo.php?lid=2748.

7.   As quoted by Stephen F. Olford, "Blow, Wind of Revival!" accessed March 9, 2017, http://www.heraldofhiscoming.com/Past%20Issues/1993/November/blow_wind_of_revival.htm.

CHAPTER 11
THE FAMINE AND THE HARVEST

1.   "10 Prophecies Fulfilled in 1948," Watchman Bible Study, accessed March 9, 2017, http://watchmanbiblestudy.com/articles/1948PropheciesFulfilled.html.

2.   "Dietrich Bonhoeffer: Costly Grace," Scroll Publishing, accessed March 9, 2017, http://www.scrollpublishing.com/store/Bonhoeffer.htm.

3.   As quoted in Ray Comfort and Kirk Cameron, *The School of Biblical Evangelism* (Alachua, FL: Bridge-Logos, 2004), 123.

CHAPTER 12
IT'S TIME TO BURN FOR HIM!

1.   John Wesley as quoted by Collegiate Wesley: United Methodist Church Student Center, accessed March 9, 2017, http://www.cwames.org/isuwesley/.

2.   Booth, as quoted in Alvin Reid, *Evangelism Handbook: Spiritual, Intentional, Missional* (Nashville: B&H Publishing Group, 2009), 285. Viewed at Google Books.

The account in 1 Kings 18 of Elijah's actions on Mount Carmel are among the most heartwarming in Scripture. Verse 30 declares, "He repaired the altar of the LORD that was broken down" (KJV). The altar has all but disappeared from the American church. God has raised Pat and Karen Schatzline up for such a time as this! Their pulpit ministry, and now this book, are undoubtedly raising awareness around the world of the importance and effectiveness of the altar.

—DON NORDIN
LEAD PASTOR, CT CHURCH
HOUSTON, TEXAS

Karen and Pat, inspired by the Lord, open our understanding to a quest for success by the presence of the Most High. With great clarity we can understand that our relationship with God can produce sweeping transformations in our lives and in our society. I am sure that God will speak in the depth of your heart, revealing and proving through this reading that it is possible to be a powerful instrument of God for this generation. The passion that characterizes Karen and Pat for a generation of fire and holiness will challenge the reader to rebuild the altar and stand as a living sacrifice to God. A must-read!

—SAMUEL VICENTE
SENIOR PASTOR
NAIC (NOVA ALIANÇA IGREJA CRISTÃ)
LISBOA, PORTUGAL

"...of the sons of Issachar who had understanding of the times, to know what Israel ought to do" (1 Chron. 12:32, NKJV). Pat and Karen have just that. They understand the now season of God. They know what our nation must do to respond to the heart of God. In their book *Rebuilding the Altar* they passionately reveal what God is saying to this nation and to His people who love this nation! Fire falls on the altar of sacrifice, and this book will cause you to return to that altar and have His fire burn within you once again! God is not a one-encounter God, and this book will cause you to return to the place of another encounter! It will cause you to say, "God, set our nation on fire once again—and let it begin with me."

—Bishop David and Pastor Kathie Thomas
Lead Pastors, Victory Christian Center
Lowellvile, Ohio

In a day and age when anything goes, this book doesn't play games with what is really important. It's not about what makes us happy or makes us feel good; it's about laying our lives down for God, dying to self. What does He want from us? When our lives are on the altar, He will alter us with His thoughts and His ways. May God use this book to stir the reader as He transforms them into His image. Thank you, Pat and Karen, for your tremendous example of two people who have laid their lives on the altar for Christ.

—Jeri Hill
Evangelist, Together in the Harvest
Gulf Shores, Alabama

As Noah stepped out of the ark, he was given an Adamic gift, a whole new world. His first act was to build an altar, then he planted vines. His work covered his altar. His son payed the price. It's time to rediscover the altar in our land and in our hearts. This new book, written from the pen of two "ready" writers, may be the axe we need. Thank you, Pat and Karen.

—Philip Cameron
Missionary, Orphan's Hands
Montgomery, Alabama

Thank you, Pat and Karen, for bringing us back to the place where we come to the end of sin and self and the beginning of God's amazing grace—the altar! *Rebuilding the Altar* is a powerful reminder that the true altar of revival is a fresh encounter with Jesus Christ and not just a physical location in a church building. As you prayerfully journey through this book, you will begin to experience new altars of awakening and freedom in your own life. You'll be reminded that your greatest need is not a new fact but a new fire—the fire that burns only on the altar!

—George Sawyer
Pastor, Calvary Assembly of God
Decatur, Alabama

Pat and Karen have written a book that is so needed, so significant for the day in which we live. I am convinced the greatest need in this hour is for men and women to have a personal, life-changing encounter with God. Pat and Karen have written a book that can show you how that can happen—a pathway to more than just an encounter, but an ongoing life lived in God's presence, flowing with God's power. You will be blessed and enriched, but also challenged to rebuild the altar of your own personal life and in your churches. I highly recommend it. It is a life-transforming book.

—Zane Anderson
Pastor, Victory Worship Center
Tucson, Arizona

Altars represent encounters with God. Prayer is not a formula to be followed but a relationship to be pursued. Broken altars mean we've outgrown our need for God encounters. Broken altars are a result of the church moving on to something more relevant and leaving a generation under the weight of unchallenged darkness. You see, "broken altars create a broken culture"! During such times God sends a prophetic cry to call His people "back to the altar"! This is what Pat and Karen have done in *Rebuilding the Altar*. This book is a call from heaven to awaken the *ecclesia* (church) to alter a nation by "rebuilding the altar"!

—Paul Owens
Pastor, Fresh Start Church
Peoria, Arizona

Having the honor to serve as youth pastor during the Brownsville Revival, where I witnessed lives being transformed nightly at the altar, I am fully convinced it is time for *Rebuilding the Altar*. Altars are more than furniture in the church; they are the encounters with God that will eradicate sin and ignite one's heart with a consuming passion for Christ. I am so glad that Pat and Karen are providing this much-needed book for this critical hour in the church.

—Richard Crisco
Lead Pastor, Rochester Christian Church
Rochester, Michigan

In their book *Rebuilding the Altar* Pat and Karen are answering the question, Can the future of the church be altered? Their answer is yes—when the believer is "altered." Their amazing revelation reveals that the only way for the church to be transformed is when the believer is transformed, and that will not happen until they are altered at the altar. The altar is our place of divine encounter. It is a place of relation, revelation, and revival. As Pat and Karen share, "God is preparing you for your 'now moment.'" Don't miss it—you'll discover it at your altar.

—KEN DRAUGHON
ALABAMA DISTRICT SUPERINTENDENT OF THE
ASSEMBLIES OF GOD
MONTGOMERY, ALABAMA

Evangelists Pat and Karen Schatzline have written a must-read for every born-again believer who desires to seek God passionately and to awaken an intimate relationship with Him. This powerful book, *Rebuilding the Altar*, is not only a how-to guide but also a cry to prepare us to experience God's divine presence continually and live in total victory. They highlight that the altar is not a place; it's a lifestyle. And they warn us that when we experience a little of God's presence, we run the risk of developing spiritual complacency. We've spent time building everything from ministries to careers. Now it's time to rebuild the altar so the Holy Spirit will fan the flames of revival once again!

—DR. RON WEBB
PASTOR, MOUNT CALVARY POWERHOUSE CHURCH
POPLAR BLUFF, MISSOURI
AUTHOR, *LEADERSHIP FROM BEHIND THE SCENES*

In this day and time rebuilding the altars is of pivotal importance. There is a powerful move of God on the horizon. Restoring the altars is a superb set of instructions on how to renew the passion for God and to restore the fire in the altars of our lives and families. I highly recommend this book from a man who not only speaks about revival but also is himself a revivalist. You will be blessed by this book.

—DR. DAVID REMEDIOS
SURGEON AND PASTOR, TRINITY CHRISTIAN CENTER
FORREST HILL, LOUISIANA

Rebuilding the Altar is a clarion call to return to a place that is more than just a particular location in a church building. It is a call to return to a spiritual place—a place of submission, a place of personal sacrifice.

—Susan Nordin
Colead Pastor, CT Church
Houston, Texas

This book is a prophetic cry for this hour, the heartbeat of a generation longing for more of God! As you read this, a "deep unto deep" moment will take place in your life. I believe you will be forever changed! Get ready for a fresh filling from God as a result of a restored radical pursuit!

—James Levesque
Pastor, Engaging Heaven Ministries
New London, Connecticut

The truth is that the altar has always been at the center of Pat's heart. You see it in his prayer life and his preaching. I can't think of anyone more qualified to express its need for resurgence.

—Dr. Patrick M. Schatzline
Founding Bishop, Daystar Ministries
International
Northport, Alabama

Truth. Clarity. Critical. These are words that come to mind when I read *Rebuilding the Altar* by my friends Pat and Karen Schatzline. The gagging and suppression of the truth has led the church into reflecting society rather than transforming it. This book is not merely "new revelation"— simply a message to flare up for a time in some readers' minds and then wither away like a fading flower. It is a shakedown of the man-infused wisdom we have allowed to penetrate the thinking of the church to the dangerous state in which we now find ourselves. Pat and Karen have taken a hammer to a lie and raised once again the unhindered, life-giving open door to the greatest invitation in all of eternity: to know God personally and responsibly make Him known. Read this before the Lord. I dare you!

—BRITT HANCOCK
MISSIONARY, MOUNTAIN GATEWAY
DRIPPING SPRINGS, TEXAS

We all know the body of Christ is in desperate need for an encounter with God. Many realize that there is within them a voice yet to shout, a warrior not yet awakened, and a cry not yet heard that will shake this world for God's glory. While many in the body of Christ know this, the revelation of how to have such an encounter with God is rarely spoken of or preached. This book is a road map that will set you on a collision course with God that will revive and restore all God has for you.

—JEREMIAH HOSFORD
PASTOR, ABUNDANT LIFE CHURCHES
JACKSON, GEORGIA

In our lifetime there has never been a more desperate hour! If there is to be anything left for the generation that follows we *must* rebuild the altar of the Lord! This book comes as a clarion call from two faithful and seasoned watchmen, Pat and Karen Schatzline. Their uncompromising and urgent message must be heard and acted upon before it is too late. Christians can no longer be halted between two opinions! We must rebuild the altar of God in our lives, lay our ambitions and agendas upon it as its sacrifice, and cry out until we are utterly consumed by His fire! I pray that as you read this incredible book, your life is forever *altared*!

—LEVI LUTZ
EVANGELIST AND FOUNDER, HARVEST NOW MINISTRIES
RUSK, TEXAS

If there's one thing I miss more than any other about the power-packed Pentecostal meetings of my childhood, it's the altar call. It was there I first received my "sight." It was there that I was filled with the Holy Spirit. It was there I first heard my call and God built a cry in me for holiness.

When I look at a largely post-Pentecostal church worldwide, it's rare to find people like Pat and Karen Schatzline who remember the altar. I believe this book and the Schatzlines' message is exactly what is needed today. Our church in San Francisco has been forever changed by their ministry, and I stand with all of heaven and applaud this call to an altar, where we finally stop the flurry of activity and take time to welcome a fresh experience of the Holy Spirit. It's time to rebuild the altars!

—Forrest Beiser
Pastor, Glad Tidings Church
San Francisco, California

Judges 2:10 says, "Another generation arose after them who did not know the Lord nor the work which He had done for Israel" (nkjv). The same can be said of the twenty-first-century church in America, Canada, and Europe. The key reason is that the church has lost sight of altar calls and altar times. In this masterful book, *Rebuilding the Altar*, Pat and Karen Schatzline give not only a prophetic insight into this lukewarm phenomenon, but they also give a "how-to," step-by-step, specific process to rebuilding the broken altars for individuals, families, the church, and the nation. Pat and Karen are needed prophetic voices to our nation and beyond. I highly recommend this must-read book.

—David A. Garcia
Pastor, Grace World Outreach Church
Brooksville, Florida

It's time for a revolution at the altar! It's time for believers and church leaders to once again prioritize our personal and public altars across America! In this riveting and convicting new book Pat and Karen Schatzline call for a fresh return to the place of the death of our flesh and the resurrection of Holy Spirit power in our lives. Get ready for revival in your life and to be "altared" by the presence of Jesus, America!

—Mark Ivey
Pastor, Christ Alive Church
Newton, North Carolina

This book will change your way of thinking about God and the altar. Romans 12:1 declares that you must "present your bodies a living sacrifice, holy, acceptable to God, which is your reasonable service" (nkjv). A living sacrifice can stay on the altar as long as it wants. Pat Schatzline told me one time, "Joe Joe, when you get done preaching and ministering in a service, don't look to talk to the people after service, but look to talk to God. Find the altar and give God all the glory. Live your life on the altar and you will reach your God-given destiny." Leviticus 6:13 says, "A fire shall always be burning on the altar; it shall never go out" (nkjv). Pat and Karen have lived this life out loud before God and a generation. Every person needs to read this book to keep the fire of God going or to help them rebuild their personal altar.

—Joe Joe Dawson
Founder and President, Burn Texarkana Revival
Center and The ROAR Apostolic Network
Texarkana, Texas

About the Authors
Pat and Karen Schatzline
Remnant Ministries International

Pat and Karen Schatzline are international evangelists and authors who co-lead Remnant Ministries International, an evangelistic ministry started in 1997 to awaken the remnant and call people of all ages back to an encounter with God. With a schedule that stays full year-round, Pat and Karen have traveled more than 2.5 million miles nationally and internationally, ministering at churches, universities, stadiums, outreaches, camps, leadership events, men's and women's conferences, and marriage retreats.

Pat and Karen's vision is to awaken the remnant and rebuild the altar, the place of encounter. To help fulfill that vision, they launched the Remnant School of Ministry, which has seen over seven hundred called into full-time ministry, and Raise the Remnant, a partnership of hundreds who connect on a weekly basis. In 2014 they launched the I Am Remnant movement, a clarion call to restore truth in all generations through the power of the Holy Spirit. Thousands have been saved, healed, and filled with the Spirit at I Am Remnant conferences held all over the nation.

Pat and Karen have appeared many times on Christian television networks such as Daystar, TBN, CTN, and JCTV, and on such TV programs as Sid Roth's *It's Supernatural!* and *The Jim Bakker Show*. Pat and Karen have written several books, including *Why Is God So Mad at Me?*, *I Am Remnant*, *Dehydrated*, and *Unqualified*. They reside in Birmingham, Alabama, with their daughter, Abigail. Their son, Nate, and daughter-in-law, Adrienne, are pastors of a thriving youth ministry in Modesto, California, and have given Pat and Karen two adorable grandsons, Jackson and Anderson.

Listen to more of Pat & Karen's Messages online via Our Podcast & Itunes

WWW.RAISETHEREMNANT.COM

WWW.REBUILDINGTHEALTAR.COM
WWW.RAISETHEREMNANT.COM
INFO@REMNANTINTL.COM
205-874-9401

Follow Pat & Karen on Twitter & Instagram:
@PatSchatz
@KarenSchatzline

Remnant
Ministries
International

CONNECT WITH US!

CHARISMA HOUSE

(Spiritual Growth)

 Facebook.com/CharismaHouse

@CharismaHouse

Instagram.com/CharismaHouse

SILOAM

(Health)

Pinterest.com/CharismaHouse

MODERN ENGLISH VERSION

(Bible)

www.mevbible.com